GETTING A

GRANT

IN THE

1990s

GETTING A
GRANT
IN THE
1990s

How to Write
Successful Grant Proposals

ROBERT LEFFERTS

PRENTICE
HALL
PRESS

NEW YORK   LONDON   TORONTO   SYDNEY   TOKYO   SINGAPORE

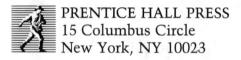 PRENTICE HALL PRESS
15 Columbus Circle
New York, NY 10023

Library of Congress Cataloging-in-Publication Data

Lefferts, Robert.
  Getting a grant in the 1990s: how to write successful grant proposals/Robert Lefferts.
  Includes bibliographical references and index.
  ISBN 0–13–313552–7 : $12.95
  Proposal writing for grants—United States—Handbooks, manuals, etc.   I. Title.
HG177.5.U6L44 1990
658.15′224—dc20   90–37223
                                                           CIP

Manufactured in the United States of America

10   9   8   7   6   5   4   3   3   2   1

First Prentice Hall Press Edition

CONTENTS

PREFACE

I BELIEVE IN PUBLICLY SHARING IDEAS AND SKILLS; TREATING IDEAS and skills as private property can be an obstacle to their use in making social progress. Unfortunately the skills related to proposal writing often have been treated as private information and have been mystified to the extent that most people are intimidated by the notion of writing a grant proposal. This book is intended to overcome this intimidation. It provides an easy-to-follow guide that any person with adequate writing skills can use to write a proposal of fundable quality.

The method used to accomplish this is called structured writing and strategic presentation. By providing a set of principles and a step-by-step outline for each part of the proposal, the writer is given a clear guide to what should appear in each section and how it should be presented in order to have the most impact on the reader. This approach, coupled with an understanding of the criteria used by funders to judge proposals, gives both the beginning and the experienced proposal writer the tools needed for confidence and success.

Earlier editions of the book, based on this same method, have been used with considerable success by thousands of students, staff people, and organization leaders in classes, institutes, and workshops. From that experience it is clear that most people already have the ability to write a good proposal. What they need is a set of guidelines, a structure, and a strategy to help translate this ability into a more effective set of skills.

Proposal writing, however, is more than a simple process in which one follows a recipe and applies a routine set of techniques. Rather, it is the integration of one's ideas with a method of presentation. No book can invent ideas for the writer. That is a matter of individual creativity. By providing the security of a structure for the proposal, however, the writer is freer to be as inventive as possible. In addition, it is important to recognize that proposal writing cannot be separated from the process of program planning and development within an organization. It is to the benefit of the organization and to the proposal writer to be sure that proposals are fully integrated with the process of program development. The only thing worse than not getting a grant is to get one that is inconsistent with the organization's mission and programmatic interests.

This edition of *Getting a Grant* incorporates the newest developments in the field of proposal writing and grant seeking based on a survey of foundations, government funding sources, and other material. A new chapter that applies the principles of marketing to the presentation of proposals has been added. Another new chapter is based on research that identified the factors most critical in keeping a grant and getting refunded. The chapter on mini-proposals and proposal letters reflects the trend among some funders to prefer briefer initial proposals. And, throughout the book the theme of being "strategic" is emphasized in order to help proposal writers capitalize on their own strengths and those of their organizations.

The book is oriented primarily to preparing program proposals in the broad field of human services including health, mental health, social welfare, education, arts and humanities, alcohol and substance abuse services, community development, housing, employment and training, and services aimed at advocacy and empowerment of groups that have been treated unfairly and have suffered the most in our society.

It is my hope that many will use this book to help obtain

resources needed in order to further their efforts to bring about an increasingly just social order in which the needs of each person are fully met regardless of social class, gender, ethnicity, race, special ability or disability, age, or life-style preference. To the extent the book is helpful to those advocating such change, my purpose will have been served. A share of the royalties from this book is donated to organizations that concern themselves with social and environmental improvements.

—Robert Lefferts
East Setauket, New York

INTRODUCTION

GETTING A GRANT IN THE 1990S COVERS THE BASIC STRUCTURE, PRIN-
ciples, and skills involved in preparing and presenting written
proposals. It is specifically directed toward proposals in the
broad field of human services including health, mental health,
social welfare, education, arts and humanities, housing, employment, and training programs. The book addresses the following questions:

- What is a proposal?
- Why are proposals increasingly important?
- What are the various types of proposals?
- What criteria are decisive in the evaluation of a proposal?
- What are the essential components of a proposal?
- What should be included in each component?
- What is the most effective form in which to present the
  material?
- What are the ways to identify potential funding sources?
- What are the best ways to approach funding sources?
- What steps can be taken to help keep a grant and obtain
  refunding?

The book is directed toward persons in nonprofit and governmental agencies, organizations, schools, and institutions as well as to community groups that are seeking financial support for special or ongoing programs, projects, services, and studies. Such financial support is typically obtained through grants and contracts from three major funding sources: private foundations, corporate funding programs, and federal, state, and local government funding agencies.

The vast majority of grants provided by foundation, corporate, and government funders are made to organizations rather than to individuals. Therefore, this book emphasizes the requirements for proposals prepared and submitted on behalf of organizations. It is estimated that more than 500,000 agencies and organizations receive in excess of $50 billion annually in grants and contracts in the fields previously noted.* Almost all of these are based on the types of proposals described in this book.

The grant marketplace is vast and complex. In recent years the number of organizations seeking grants has greatly increased, resulting in a concomitant rise in competition. In addition, allocating agencies have become more sophisticated and critical in their proposal assessment. They have developed criteria and review methods enabling them to examine proposals much more critically. All of these factors have resulted in what is known as a more "elastic" funding market, characterized by considerable choice on the part of funders as to where they will allocate their money. In this situation, the written proposal takes on increased importance as a critical factor in making judgments regarding fund allocation. However, the quality of the proposal is not the only factor taken into consideration in awarding a grant. Political, personal, public relations, financial, and ideological factors influence decision making in foundations and government funding agencies, just as they influence decision making in all other realms of American life. Proposal writing and grant seeking are not activities that rely alone on the operation of a meritocracy. For this reason, one can receive endless and often contradictory advice from "experts" on how

---

*Most of this money is in governmental grants. The total amount granted from foundations is about $7 billion; another $5 billion comes from corporate sources. One half of corporate giving is to educational institutions.

to obtain a grant. However, one thing is clear: Getting a grant depends on a written proposal, and the quality of the proposal and how it is presented is a critical factor in obtaining a grant.

Proposal writing is part technical craft and part art. There are many ways to organize a proposal. Every proposal writer develops his or her own style and method of presentation. It is not the purpose of this book to make all proposals look alike or to reduce the creativity involved in writing a proposal. There is no surefire set of instructions to guarantee a good proposal. Nevertheless, a certain structure and some tried-and-true principles and methods can help refine one's ability to prepare a more convincing proposal. And one must adhere to certain requirements of funders in order to be competitive.

In addition to the necessity of preparing a high-quality proposal, organizations seeking grants must be able to identify the appropriate funders to whom the proposal should be submitted. Perhaps no division of the nonprofit sector is characterized by a greater proliferation of potential resources than the grant-making field. More than 27,000 private foundations and thousands of federal, state, and local government agencies provide grants in this field. Moreover, thousands of corporations provide grants in the form of corporate gifts and foundations for public service programs, research, and training. In the face of this situation proposal writers must develop guidelines for making decisions as to where to seek funds. In the last ten years a great many books and consulting organizations have come into being in order to help identify potential funding agencies. These resources are reviewed in this book and suggestions for their use are also included. In addition, certain principles and methods to help the grant seeker deal with the confusing and often frustrating problem of identifying potential funders are outlined.

Finally, one of the themes throughout this book is the importance of developing a strategic approach to proposal writing and grant seeking. Such a strategy involves not only assessing the potential funding marketplace but also identifying your own strengths and weaknesses as a proposal writer and as a grant-seeking organization. All of us have certain strengths, and the effective proposal writer is one who knows how to capitalize on these strengths and how to minimize weaknesses. This book will help you do both.

1

WHAT IS A PROPOSAL?

UNDERSTANDING WHAT A PROPOSAL REPRESENTS HELPS US TO FOCUS on certain basic principles of proposal writing. Webster defines a proposal as a plan presented for acceptance. The word itself comes from the Latin *pro*, which means "for" or "in favor of"; and from the French *poser*, which means "to set forth." Importantly then, a proposal must be a positive statement, never a negative one. And, it must be a positive statement that sets forth an activity or program in such a way that its chances of being accepted are maximized.

Effective proposals use positive language to describe their activities in a convincing manner. One cannot really make a proposal *against* something. A proposal is always *for* something. Even a counterproposal, which may be directed in opposition to some idea or activity, is always stated as a positive assertion of an alternative idea or action.

A proposal always requires two parties. A proposal is made by one party to another party who either accepts, rejects, or modifies it. Thus, when writing a proposal, it is important to focus on the fact that it is being written for the sole purpose of

1

presenting it to someone else to convince them to accept the proposal. This does not mean that one must compromise one's values and principles in order to please a funder. But it does mean that the presentation must be sufficiently clear, appealing, and persuasive to be convincing. It also means that the language and style must be understandable to the funder to whom the proposal is being submitted. In addition, the proposal must be in tune with the needs and interests of the funder to whom it is being sent. Fortunately, the great majority of funders express their interests in sufficiently broad and clear terms so that most proposal writers can present grant proposals consistent with the funders' interests. Chapters 4 and 7 discuss how to do this.

A proposal serves four main functions: It is (1) a program plan, (2) a request, (3) a promise, and (4) an instrument of persuasion. Each of these functions has certain implications for the preparation and presentation of the proposal, as outlined below.

PROGRAM PLAN

A proposal is a written statement that represents a particular program or project an organization would like to undertake. As such, it is part of the process of program planning, program development, and resource acquisition. To the organization presenting the proposal it represents a set of guidelines for implementing the program. To the funder it is an indication of the organization's program-planning ability. It is important, therefore, that the proposal clearly indicate all of the major activities that will be carried out and how they will be organized and implemented. Therefore the proposal writer must have a good understanding of how to organize the program and the various steps required to implement it successfully. In addition, the number and type of staff needed, how they will be organized, how the program will be managed, the equipment required, the completion time for each activity, and the costs involved should all be described as part of a sound program plan. Since the proposal sets forth the various activities of the planned program it also can be a tool to use in managing the program as it is being implemented. A good proposal reflects good program planning.

A REQUEST

The second function of a proposal is that it represents a request for the allocation of financial resources from the funding source, which means that the proposal should clearly indicate the exact amount of money being requested, what specific items the money will be spent for, and a justification of the need for each major item.

Because a proposal "asks" for something, many proposal writers have difficulty handling this aspect of the proposal. They are uncomfortable asking for money, and they feel subservient to the funder. If this feeling is reflected in the tone of the proposal or the letter submitting the proposal, the proposal can be less effective. The tone and style of the proposal must command the respect and attention of the funder. Proposals that have a "please give us the money" or a begging tone are not going to be respected by the funder, since they give the impression that the applicant may not be sure of the value of the proposed work. On the other hand, proposals that have a "we are entitled to the money" or an arrogant tone are also to be avoided since they can negate the kind of mutuality of interest and working relationship that funders prefer. The proposal should be straightforward in describing the work that will be done and the necessary budget requirements.

A PROMISE

The third function of a proposal is that it is a promise. The applicant makes a commitment to the funder that certain things will be done during a specified time period at a certain cost. Frequently, especially if federal, state, or local governmental agencies are involved, the proposal is made part of a legal contract. Failure to perform in accordance with the proposal can result in a loss of funding. In addition to the proposal itself, funders may impose their own conditions and expectations to which the applicant must adhere. In effect, the proposal is a written statement of the work to be performed in exchange for the funds received. Funders may require periodic progress reports detailing changes in the originally proposed program, modifications in the budget, or other conditions that were not in the original proposal. Any changes, once the funds are accepted, should be taken seriously by an applicant.

In view of the potentially binding nature of a proposal, great care should be taken not to promise what cannot be delivered. One of the most frequent mistakes made by proposal writers is to overpromise what the proposed activity will accomplish or the scope of activities that will be undertaken.

In addition, when accepting funds from governmental funders the applicant often must agree to many legal provisions beyond the proposal itself, including rules regarding equal opportunity employment and affirmative action programs, approval for program, budget, and personnel changes, provisions regarding the protection of human subjects in research projects, and the like.

PERSUASION

The fourth function of a proposal is that it is an instrument of persuasion. Through the proposal we seek to persuade some person or organization to support the proposed activity by allocating funds to the applicant. In addition to providing money, the funding foundation or government agency also lends its name to the project, thereby helping to legitimate the project. Money and legitimation are not easily disbursed, and funders need to be wholly convinced that their support should be granted. In this sense the proposal is also a political document since it is aimed at convincing another party, that is, the funder, to become an ally.

In the process of persuasion some proposal writers may view

funders as adversaries, at least until they come through with the sought-after grant. Writers may also think that funders are going to be unsympathetic to the approach they may be taking to provide a particular program. Experience has shown that these notions are not well founded. In general, chances of persuading a funder to approve a proposal are improved by being straightforward in describing the nature of the proposed program. It is not advisable to try to psych out the politics of a funder. What appear to be conservative funders have often supported progressive or "radical" programs. Funding sources that appear to be liberal support conservative programs. Whatever the politics of a proposed program, avoid rhetorical, provocative, or inflammatory language. Facts and documentation should be stressed. Aspects of the proposal that challenge accepted ideas and practices should be described clearly and precisely in a low-key manner. Do not hesitate to challenge conventional ideas, since this is the essence of innovation. And innovation is of great importance to many funders.

The importance of well-written proposals cannot be stressed too strongly. In general, one out of every ten of the millions of proposals submitted each year will receive funding. The quality of the proposal can provide the difference between being accepted or rejected.

Different people begin the proposal-writing process in different ways, depending on their own approach to problem solving, decision making, planning, and writing. Some people start with a general idea, concept, or purpose and then make it more specific. This method is called deductive thinking. Others prefer to start with a specific program activity or idea and expand it into an overall concept, plan, and set of objectives. This method is called inductive thinking. Most proposal writers actually go back and forth from the general to the specific, from the specific to the general. This means that during preparation one should expect to revise the proposal several times. Experienced and successful writers almost all say that part of their key to success is in the revision process. In addition, when the proposal is finally completed, it should be carefully reviewed to be sure that it meets the criteria described in chapter 3. Finally, it should be edited for grammar, punctuation, internal consistency, and clarity.

This book provides guidelines for proposal writing that can be used with both deductive and inductive approaches. Before describing these guidelines, it is helpful to understand the different types of proposals and the criteria used by funders to assess proposals. All of these topics are covered in the next two chapters.

2

TYPES OF
PROPOSALS

THERE ARE MANY DIFFERENT TYPES OF PROPOSALS AND THE REQUIRE-
ments for each differ somewhat. In addition, funders may only
support certain kinds of proposals and not others. It is important to understand the variations among proposals and to select
funders that support the particular type of proposal that you
develop.

There are six major types of proposals in the health and human services fields:

- *Program proposals.* To provide one or more services to
  individuals, families, groups, or communities

- *Research proposals.* To study a problem, group of people,
  or organization; or, to evaluate a service or program

- *Training proposals.* To offer training and educational programs to individuals, groups, organizations, or communities

- *Planning proposals.* To provide planning, coordination,
  and networking in connection with a problem or among a
  group of organizations or programs

- *Technical assistance proposals.* To provide assistance to groups, agencies, and organizations in developing, implementing, and managing programs, studies, or other activities
- *Capital improvement proposals.* To build or remodel buildings and acquire equipment

Since the vast majority of proposals submitted are program proposals, these are used as the model in this book. In addition, because research proposals have special characteristics, chapter 6 is devoted exclusively to them. Guidelines with respect to training, planning, and technical assistance proposals are essentially the same as for program proposals.

Few foundations or government funding programs will grant money for capital improvements. Those that do often have special requirements that should be obtained from those funders.

Any particular proposal may, of course, include a combination of two or more of the types of proposals described above. For example, a proposal may include a set of counseling and treatment services for persons abusing alcohol as well as a training program for alcohol-counselor staff members. A program proposal to provide nutrition services to older people may also contain an evaluation of those services, which is a form of research. A program proposal aimed at establishing a new program for pregnant teenagers may include an initial set of activities devoted to planning the new program.

Regardless of the type of proposal being prepared, the same general principles apply, but the specifics will differ somewhat. For example, every proposal should have a section describing exactly what will be done with the funds received. In a program proposal this information is covered in a section describing each program activity that will be carried out and the number and characteristics of the people who will be served. A research proposal covers the same general information in a section on research design that explains what data will be collected and what research methods will be used to collect and analyze the data.

SPECIAL PROJECT OR ONGOING ACTIVITY?

A major distinction made by funders is whether a proposal is for a special project or for the support of the organization's regular or ongoing operating program. A project is usually presented as a new set of services that will be provided or as an extension of services to an entirely new group of people or community. Sometimes projects are presented as demonstrations or pilot programs. Many funders do not provide support for regular program operations or what are referred to as "regular operating expenses." Indeed there is a debate in the funding community over the extent to which foundations should or should not limit their support to special projects. Thus, it is important to determine the limitations of any potential funding source in this regard and prepare the proposal accordingly. On a few occasions this may necessitate "repackaging" some regular activities in order to meet the requirements of a particular funder. In general, the proposal writing strategy here is to make it evident that the proposed activities are a significant departure from or addition to the routine activities of the organization. When referring to the proposed activities as a pilot program or a demonstration, it is essential to show that the methods or strategies being proposed will be tested to determine their effectiveness, efficiency, strengths, and weaknesses. Further, there should be a plan for dissemination of the results of a pilot or demonstration program. Implicit in proposals for projects, pilots, and demonstrations is that they have a time limit, and the proposal should include an explanation of intended limits.

SOLICITED OR UNSOLICITED

A proposal may be solicited or unsolicited. A solicited proposal is prepared in response to a formal written *request for proposals* known as an RFP. In addition, proposals may be solicited or invited by program announcements or program guidelines sent out by funders to describe the availability of funds for various purposes. RFPs and other announcements inviting proposals by government agencies are included in the *Commerce Business Daily*, a government publication that covers all federal funding programs. RFPs are usually very detailed and may specify the length of the proposal, the topics to be covered, the manner in which the budget is to be submitted and the like. Proposals prepared in response to an RFP or program announcement must be carefully checked to be sure they adhere to all of the funder's specifications. If they do not, the proposal has little chance of being successful.

The majority of proposals are unsolicited. These are not prepared in response to a formal RFP or invitation to submit proposals; rather, the proposal is initiated by the organization seeking support and then sent to the foundations and government agencies known to support that kind of proposed program. There is usually more latitude in the form and content of unsolicited proposals. Many foundations have requirements regarding the form and content of proposals sent to them and these requirements can be obtained ahead of time by requesting them of the foundation. The requirements will seldom be as stringent as those included in RFPs.

TECHNICAL AND BUSINESS PROPOSALS

Most government funders and a few foundations make a distinction between "technical" proposals and "business" proposals. The technical proposal includes all of the information describing the program's objectives, activities, methods, organization, and staffing pattern. The business proposal includes the budget, pricing, and all other financial information. Sometimes these are referred to as Part I and Part II of the proposal and may be reviewed and evaluated separately by the funder.

OPERATING OR CAPITAL

Proposals may seek to cover either the costs of operating a program or the costs for capital expenses ranging from construction and renovation of buildings to the acquisition of major pieces of equipment. While most funders allow the costs of buying or renting equipment directly related to program operations (such as typewriters and chairs), most will not pay for new or renovated building expenses. Equipment such as computers and photocopying machines may be funded by some (often on a rental basis for expensive equipment) and may be disallowed by others. Proposals for capital improvements and acquisition of equipment should be selectively submitted to the relatively few foundations and government programs that specifically support such expenditures. Resources for identifying these funding sources are described in chapter 8.

SOLE SOURCE

Occasionally an organization will have a unique capability to carry out a program and will be selected by a funder as the so-called sole source to receive a contract. In such a case there is no competition with other organizations, but a proposal acceptable to the funder must still be prepared.

GRANTS AND CONTRACTS

Foundations, government agencies, and other funding sources support organizations in two ways: through either grants or contracts. Both of these support mechanisms are used to define the conditions, requirements, and expectations under which the funds are made available by the funder. Thus, they guide both the nature and extent of the relationship between the funder and the recipient.

Some significant differences between grants and contracts not only influence the proposal's content but also affect the manner in which funds must be managed after they are awarded and received. Contracts tend to be much more specific about how and what particular services will be provided. Contracts also specify what final results or products are expected. These products or deliverables may be in the form of reports, or numbers of people served, or number of service units (e.g., counseling sessions) to be provided. If a proposal is in response to a formal RFP, the award will usually be made in the form of a contract. Contracts are used frequently by federal, state, and local government funders.

Most foundations support programs with grants. In these cases, there is no formal contract to sign, although there may be a letter of agreement. Grant awards are commonly communicated by letter and may specify the general services to be provided but seldom do they specify final products in the way a contract does. In the case of both grants and contracts, the proposal you submit will usually be a part of the understanding reached with the funder.

When applying for funds to be awarded in the form of a contract, it is usually necessary to complete a number of different forms covering both program and financial information. In the case of grants, especially from foundations, a narrative proposal, a budget, and tax exemption letter from the IRS are sufficient and there are seldom many forms to fill out. For contracts from federal, state, and local government agencies, the main forms used include program descriptions, financial information, and certificates and assurances that certain employment, administrative, and business procedures and practices will be followed. Samples of these are shown in chapter 4.

Many proposal writers and administrators believe that, from the standpoint of the grantee, a grant is preferable to a contract. Theoretically, a grant provides more flexibility for the grantee since it is less specific regarding the products and the conditions under which the supported activities will be undertaken. In addition, there is often less monitoring by the funder of a grant than there is of a contract. Note that although this is generally the case, there is also a good deal of variability in actual practice; occasionally contracts result in as much, if not more, flexibility than a grant.

Many different kinds of contracts and grants are used by funders to convey funds to grantees. These mechanisms provide for different conditions under which the funds are made available and different conditions regarding how the funds may be expended. Contracts take many forms, including cost-plus, cost-reimbursable, and cost-sharing contracts. Grants are classified according to their purpose such as program grants, planning grants, training grants, construction grants, and grants-in-aid. The differences among these contract and grant mechanisms are defined in the Glossary.

3

CRITERIA FOR
EVALUATING
PROPOSALS

MOST FUNDING SOURCES, INCLUDING ALMOST ALL FEDERAL AGENCIES, apply formal criteria in evaluating proposals. One can use these same criteria for self-evaluation of the proposal prior to its submission to a funder. A funder may be requested to provide the criteria and priority statements used, since these are usually public information.

The criteria used by funders vary, of course; however, the following list represents those most frequently used. Sometimes they are applied very formally and points are awarded for each criterion when the proposal is evaluated. For example, the criterion of clarity may be worth 25 points and each proposal received is given up to 25 points, depending on the judgment of the individual or panel that reviews it. In other cases the criteria are not made explicit and are not applied formally but are simply guidelines in the mind of the reviewers.

One can evaluate his or her own proposal against the following nine criteria:

Clarity
Completeness

Responsiveness
Internal consistency
External consistency
Understanding of the problem and service methods
Capability and effectiveness
Efficiency and accountability
Realism

These criteria are explained in a general way below. Remember that, when applied by a specific funder to a specific proposal, they are used in a more specific sense. For example, if the proposal is for a program in the area of drug abuse prevention, the funder wants the applicant to demonstrate an understanding of the specifics of the drug abuse problem and of the delivery of services or conduct of research in this field.

CLARITY

The proposal must be clearly written and organized so that it can be readily followed and easily understood. The style of writing and organization of material should be as simple as possible. Complicated sentence structure, verbiage, abstractions not clarified with examples, long sentences, and a great deal of cross-referencing should be avoided.

It is important to avoid jargon whose meaning is ambiguous, but one should use a certain amount of the generally understood technical or professional language relevant to the proposal. One should be convinced, however, that the funding reviewers also are familiar with this language and use it.

Clarity is enchanced by a logical flow of ideas and by the use of headings and subheadings that break up the text and also describe to the reader what he or she is reading. Use them!

It cannot be assumed that the funder will understand what is intended unless the proposal includes a full explanation. The writer has to ask "Will someone unfamiliar with my organization have a *clear picture* of what is being proposed from reading the proposal?" After the proposal is complete, one must identify what kinds of questions a funder may ask about the proposal and have two or three other people review it critically. Thereupon the proposal should be revised to cover the answers to the anticipated questions.

In the words of one foundation:

> There is no substitute for clarity and simplicity. Unless your project deals with highly technical matters, there is probably no reason for you to use professional jargon or "buzz words" in the proposal. Jargon usually succeeds in only muddying the flow of your argument and does your project a disservice. Keep in mind that many of the men and women who will read and evaluate your project have no experience in your field.

COMPLETENESS

The proposal must include all the components and elements outlined in chapter 4. If the proposal is being written in response to a request for proposals (RFP), a request for applications (RFA), program announcement, regulations, or guidelines one should be sure that it covers every item specified. Be sure that all forms are completed and the IRS tax exemption letter is included, if required. It should cover all relevant points, so that the funding agency does not have any major unanswered questions about purpose, objectives, need, activities, staffing, organization, timing, or budget request. Use of the words "etc." or "and so forth" must be avoided, since this may be construed to indicate that the writer really does not know the complete range of material to be presented.

One federal agency stresses the importance of completeness thus:

> Your application must include *all* necessary information and materials. Required signatures, letters of agreement . . . , etc. must be included. Please remember that *no* additional materials can be accepted after the relevant submission deadline or considered in the review, unless specifically requested by the Executive Secretary of the Initial Review Group.

RESPONSIVENESS

Proposals must be responsive to the requirements and interests of the funding agency and must also be responsive to a documented problem and need.

RESPONSIVENESS TO FUNDING AGENCY REQUIREMENTS AND INTERESTS

Proposals to government funding agencies must be responsive to all the substantive specifications regarding both format and content set forth in the RFP, program announcement, guidelines, regulations, and legislation relevant to the program under which funding is sought. They must also be responsive to the general interests and purposes of the funder to whom they are submitted. The information needed to assure that a proposal is responsive to these requirements is provided by examination of the legislative authority, rules, regulations, program guidelines, goals, and objectives of the governmental funding programs concerned.

Some foundations also have written guidelines that proposals must meet. In addition, information to enhance responsiveness to the interests of a particular foundation can be provided by examining foundation annual reports and other materials. These reports and guidelines can be obtained by simply calling or writing the foundation office. Many are available in the Foundation Center Library, which has offices in New York City and other cities throughout the country. These are listed in the Appendix. Corporate funders also have special interests, and corporate grants are made to reflect favorably on the corporation. Proposals to corporations should, therefore, show a connection between the proposed project and the interests of the corporation and its employees.

RESPONSIVENESS TO NEED

The proposal should also demonstrate that it is responding to a real and documented need or problem in the community, among the group to be served, and/or in the general field. This need should be comprehensively documented, following the guidelines in chapter 4. The proposal will be strengthened by showing that the proposed program is responsive to the interests of those who will be involved. Letters of endorsement, the results of surveys, community meetings, and waiting lists can serve to document responsiveness to need.

INTERNAL CONSISTENCY

All parts of the proposal should be related to and consistent with each other. For example, the activities proposed should be logically consistent with the objectives set forth. Similarly, the proposed staff should be of sufficient size and quality to deliver the proposed services. Statements about need should be directly relevant to the specific program activities being proposed.

EXTERNAL CONSISTENCY

The proposal should recognize both the generally known and accepted ideas in the particular field and the program approaches, activities, and methods that are believed to be effective. If alternative definitions of the problem and alternative service strategies and methods are proposed, they should be justified in terms of a systematic critique of the dominant ideas and methods. This, in effect, is a way to enhance the innovative aspects of the proposal and to demonstrate, at the same time, familiarity with the field.

UNDERSTANDING OF THE PROBLEM AND SERVICE METHODS

It is important to indicate a thorough understanding of the nature of the problem that the program addresses. In addition, the proposal should show one's understanding of the way in which the proposed services must be delivered. Most importantly, it must have an effective plan to carry out the proposed activities. A proposal is also strengthened by indicating that one understands the barriers, problems, and difficulties that must be overcome in order to provide the proposed services effectively and achieve the objectives.

CAPABILITY AND EFFECTIVENESS

A major criterion to funders is evidence of the capability of the organization to successfully carry out the activities it promises to implement in its written proposal. This can be conveyed in a number of ways, particularly by the quality of the proposal itself and by demonstrating familiarity with the problem, the relevant literature, the service-delivery methods, and other similar programs. Setting forth the qualifications of the proposed staff or the experience and resources of the agency involved is likewise important in emphasizing capability. Funders are usually concerned with the applicant's prior work or "track record" of successful operation.

It is often advisable to include a separate "capability statement" with the proposal. This should take the form of an attachment or appendix. Letters of endorsement from key organizations and authorities may also be attached and referred to in the proposal. Finally, evidence of the applicant's plans and ability to assure continuance and funding of the project in the future conveys capability to a funder.

EFFICIENCY AND ACCOUNTABILITY

Funders want assurance that programs will be efficiently managed and effectively executed. Plans for the administration and organization of the program activities, staff, and committees are ways to indicate ability to implement the program efficiently. Assurance of accountability to the community, a larger institution, and the funder are other factors that enhance efficiency. A detailed timetable is important as well. Other ways to stress efficiency are to compare the cost of the program with the cost of alternative programs; to indicate the cost of the problem to the community; and to show a favorable relationship between the budgeted expenses and the activities for the number of people to be served (the so-called unit costs).

The accountability factor of the proposal can be strengthened by indicating the kinds of managerial and financial systems and controls that will be employed; by showing how advisory boards and committees will be utilized; and by providing a description of regular reports to the membership, other institutions, and the funder.

REALISM

A proposal should be realistic. Promise no more than can really be achieved and delivered in the way of objectives and program activities. The proposal should be geared to the realities of the number of people that can actually be served.

The dollar request must be consistent with the amount of money available from the funder. Chapters 7 and 8 suggest certain specific resources and techniques for making a realistic assessment of potential resources.

For additional reading about the foregoing criteria we suggest the following articles of the *Grantsmanship Center News* (1015 West Olympic Boulevard, Los Angeles, California 90015): "How Foundations Review Proposals and Make Grants," "Researching Foundations," and "An Inside Look at How the Government Evaluates Proposals."

A number of ideas relevant to foundation proposals have been set forth by F. Lee Jacquette and Barbara I. Jacquette, in "What Makes a Good Proposal." (Reprints are available from the Foundation Center.) This article is specifically geared to proposals submitted to foundations. It stresses the need for a clear summary of the proposed accomplishment, an explanation of the need for the proposed program and of its difference from programs worked out by others, a description of the people to be involved including their biographies and qualifications, presentation of a realistic financing scheme and of an appropriate set of organizational arrangements. According to this article, most foundations assess proposals using the following criteria:

Competence of persons involved
Feasibility and realism of the proposal
Importance and usefulness of the venture to the community or to society
Originality and creativity of the proposed venture
Appropriateness of the project to the foundation's policy and program focus
Prospects for leverage and pattern-making effects
Need for foundation support
Soundness of the budget
Persistence, dedication, and commitment of the proposers
Provision of objective evaluation of results, where feasible

Another helpful article is "What Will a Foundation Look for When You Submit a Grant Proposal" by Robert A. Mayer. (It too is available from the Foundation Center.) Mayer says that foundation staff members look for the following in a proposal:

- Does the proposal fit within the foundation's program interests?

- Is the type of support requested of the kind the foundation gives (for example, the covering of operating deficits, construction, or special projects)?

- Does the project have value, a transferral potential, an impact on need, or an intrinsic value of its own from which others might benefit?

- Is it aimed at building organizations in areas in which the foundation has institution-building purposes?

- Is the cost, timetable, and future financing plan realistic?

- Does the organization have the leadership, experience, and resources to accomplish the objectives?

Some funders use a very brief and rather specific set of criteria upon which they base their assessment of a proposal. For example, one crime grant program listed the following criteria:

Clear definition of objectives

Crime-analysis data on the community that demonstrate a need for the program

Endorsement of the proposal by the local police department

Demonstrable coordination and involvement of the police in the program

Specific qualifications of the applicant to perform the projects

Another federal program indicated it rates proposals according to the following criteria:

1. Needs and objectives—0 to 10 points
2. Evidence of private sector involvement—0 to 30 points
3. Cost-effectiveness and reasonableness—0 to 10 points
4. Demand for occupational choices identified for training—0 to 20 points
5. Ability of applicant to provide effective programming—0 to 30 points

From experience with government and foundation reviewers it is evident that, in addition to the general criteria outlined earlier, reviewers also tend to look for a number of more specific items in a proposal. These include:

The importance or significance of the project in terms of documented need, the extent to which the project will meet this need, and the number and characteristics of the people to be served.

The extent to which the project involves the cooperation of other community resources, both public and private, and evidence that duplication and overlapping of services is avoided.

The specificity with which objectives are set forth and the suitability of the proposed methods or activities as means to accomplish the objectives.

The clear description of the proposed tasks and the competence of the proposers to make good on their promises.

The suitability and soundness of proposed evaluation techniques, particularly in terms of the kinds of measurements that will be made, the feasibility of obtaining data adequate for making such measurements, and clarity with respect to the question of which specific evaluation issues will and which will not be answered as a result of the evaluation. Program-proposal writers tend to hedge more in relationship to evaluation than to any other section of the proposal, and reviewers recognize this.

The evidence that the proposed project has a relationship to other local, state, or national programs with which the government funding agency also has a relationship or interest.

The possibility that the proposed program can be sold by reviewers to other officials in the funding agency who also need to approve it.

The reasonableness of the budget, its technical presentation and accuracy, and the probability of continuing support. An increasing amount of attention is given to judgments about the relationship of costs to benefits and effectiveness. These judgments are made in terms of whether unit costs are reasonable and in line with similar programs, and whether the proposed program is worth its costs in relation to the probability of achieving its program objectives and its impact on the problem.

A variety of forms and instructions is used among governmental proposal reviewers. Often reviewers are asked to make a general rating or recommendation regarding each proposal such as approve, approve with provisions or qualifications, disapprove, or defer action. Reviewers also rate various aspects of the proposal awarding points or using scales. For example, reviewers may be asked to rate "the significance of the problem addressed" on a five-point scale of 1 to 5; similarly, other aspects, such as the adequacy of procedures and methods, the qualifications of staff, and the extent to which budget costs are proportionate to expected results may be rated on point scales.

In preparing a proposal, the writer should have all the foregoing criteria and questions in mind and should reexamine each component of the proposal to see if it can be strengthened to more nearly conform to these criteria.

Proposal writers should not be overly mystified or overwhelmed by these criteria. For one thing, they are really not that complicated, since they all reflect commonsense questions, which anyone would ask when faced with making a decision about providing resources to another party. In addition, the decision-making process among funding agencies is not always as orderly, technical, and rational as the discussion of criteria might imply or as funders' formal descriptions of their decision-making process may sound. A good deal of personal judgment, not reflected in formal criteria but rather based on values and politics affecting the funder, can come into play.

4

COMPONENTS OF A PROPOSAL

A COMPLETE PROPOSAL MAY HAVE AS MANY AS FOURTEEN COMPO-
nents, including:

- Letter of Transmittal
- Title Page
- Headings and Table of Contents
- Summary
- Introduction
- Purpose and Objectives
- Problem Definition and Need
- Frame of Reference or Rationale
- Description of Program Activities
- Organizational Structure, Administration, and Staffing
- Timetable
- Evaluation Plan
- Budget and Budget Explanation
- Capability Statement

The principles and methods to guide the preparation and presentation of each of these components will be taken up in-

dividually in the following sections of this chapter. Many government funding programs require submission of a proposal using their own forms and outlines, and some samples of these are included. In addition, a few foundations and corporate funders have their own application formats. Most limit themselves to suggesting a general outline that, in the majority of cases, corresponds to the components described in this chapter. The terminology used by funding agencies varies greatly. In addition, they may ask that the material be presented in a different order from that being used in this chapter. Similarly, different proposal writers and authorities in the field have had success using different formats to organize the material. The most important of these variations, differences in terminology, and organization, are pointed out in the discussion of each component.

The question often raised is, "What is the most important part of the proposal?" Naturally, all parts of the proposal are important since a proposal can be rejected because of a weakness in any one section. Nevertheless, studies of funders indicate that some weaknesses show up more frequently than others. Two particular problems stand out. First, the proposal often fails to show an adequate understanding of the problem it seeks to address and does not provide enough or convincing evidence that the proposed program activities (or research design) will be effective. Second, the proposal and the information about the applicant do not provide the funder with sufficient confidence in the competence of the applicant to carry out the activity successfully. This suggests that the program description section of the proposal and the staffing and capability sections are often where proposal writers run into the most trouble. It is not, as many proposal writers believe, the budget request that is the biggest problem.

In addition to the foregoing, many proposals are weakened because certain kinds of mistakes are made in different sections of the proposal. These mistakes, most of which are avoidable, tend to erode the funder's confidence in the proposal. Thus, in the material that follows, we will not only present sound principles and methods of proposal preparation but also will call attention to the more frequent errors made by proposal writers.

LETTER OF TRANSMITTAL

The letter of transmittal or cover letter formally submits the proposal to the funder. It should include:

- Name, address, and phone number of the organization transmitting the proposal
- What the proposal is about including a concise summary of the problem, need, objectives, and program approach
- Why the proposal is being sent to this particular funder
- Brief statement of the organization's interest in the project and its capability and experience
- Who to contact for additional information and an indication of the willingness to provide more information

The letter of transmittal is usually the first part of the proposal that the funder sees and reads. It can set the tone for the way the reviewer considers the remainder of the proposal. It should be brief, clear, neat, and properly addressed. It should be double-checked to be sure the name and title of the person to whom it is being sent is correct. Call the funder to confirm this if necessary.

In a few cases, federal RFPs may require information regarding who prepared the proposal and for what period of time the proposal and budget can be considered as a firm commitment from the organization. Some government and foundation forms and outlines do not require a letter of transmittal, but it is usually a good idea to include one.

The letter should be on the organization's letterhead stationery. The letterhead should not be elaborate, but should convey confidence by indicating that the organization is incorporated, listing the board of directors, and showing any important affiliations with a larger or national organization. Avoid using shaded paper for the letterhead (and for the proposal itself) unless you are sure it will photocopy without any problem. The letter should be signed by the chief officer of the organization and include the title that shows his or her authority.

How long should the letter be? Most cover letters are one or two pages. If the proposal is short, that is, less than eight pages,

April 12, 1990

Ms. Mary Smith, Executive Director
Famous Foundation
One Washington Street
Anywhere, Ohio 99911

Dear Ms. Smith:

The ABC Organization is pleased to submit the enclosed proposal to provide a drug abuse prevention program for teenage youth in Somewhere, Illinois. This program is consistent with the goal of your foundation to support alternative programs for youth. The purpose of the program is to demonstrate the effectiveness of a comprehensive program of health, education, training, and social services in reducing the incidence and prevalence of drug abuse among teenagers who have a high risk of using dangerous addictive substances.

The program, which has been endorsed by the police department and the public schools, will be aimed at youth who have dropped out of school and have come to the attention of the police. Studies have shown that this group, of whom there are some 1500 a year in Somewhere, are those who have the highest risk for use of illegal addictive substances.

The program will be an alternative to having these youths enter the criminal justice system. Our program will divert youth from the generally unsatisfactory effects of institutionalization and provide them with a set of activities to increase their marketable skills, enhance their self-esteem, and improve their physical well-being. The program is described in detail in the proposal. One of the main features of the program will be the use of peer support groups and involvement of youth in community service projects as ways to open up new patterns of peer-related behavior.

The ABC Organization has a record of successfully serving youth since 1957. Operating through three community centers with a total budget of $2 million from government contracts and foundation grants, we have demonstrated new approaches to serving young unwed mothers, young mental patients, and abused children through a number of projects described in the capability statement attached to the proposal. Our highly qualified staff and representative Board of Directors are all committed to providing new services to meet emerging needs in the community.

The enclosed proposal outlines, in detail, the need, objectives, program activities, staffing, management plan, timetable, and budget for the proposed program. We would be glad to discuss this proposal with you and to provide any additional information you may want. We shall look forward to hearing from you.

Sincerely yours,

Virginia Jones, President

enc.

Figure 1. Sample letter of transmittal.

the letter should be about one page and contain only one or two paragraphs summarizing the proposal. If the proposal is longer, then the letter can be longer and include a more complete summary of the proposal. A summary section should also be included in the body of a long proposal, because the letter may not be seen by all of the persons that the funder may have reviewing the proposal.

Figure 1 is a sample letter of transmittal.

TITLE PAGE

A separate title page or cover greatly enhances the appearance of a proposal, adds to its credibility, and increases its impact on the reader. The title page should include:

- The title of the proposal
- A descriptive subtitle if necessary
- Name and address of the organization submitting the proposal
- Date
- Name of the funding agency or organization to whom the proposal is being submitted

Some proposal writers also show the amount of money being requested on the title page as well as the scheduled dates for

---

Proposal to Establish
A Drug Abuse Prevention Program
For Teenage Youth

Submitted to
The Famous Foundation
by the
ABC Organization
2 Lincoln Avenue
Somewhere, Illinois 22222

April 1990

Total Request $200,000

Figure 2. Sample title page.

the start and end of the proposed project. Figure 2 is a sample title page.

If a title that is used is an acronym (i.e., made up of a combination of the first letters of each word in the title), a descriptive subtitle should always be given. Also, avoid a nondescriptive title such as OPERATION HELP since it by itself does not provide any clear indication of what the proposal is about. A subtitle, such as "A Self-Help Program For School Dropouts," clarifies the project's purpose. The more direct, clear, and descriptive the title is, the better. Avoid decorating the title page with elaborate borders or designs. Don't be tempted to use them just because you have a computer program with this capability. A simple heavy line at the top and bottom of the page, as shown in Figure 2, is enough in the way of design and sets off the text nicely.

OMB Approval No. 29-R0218

FEDERAL ASSISTANCE

1. TYPE OF ACTION (Mark appropriate box)	☐ PREAPPLICATION ☐ APPLICATION ☐ NOTIFICATION OF INTENT (Opt.) ☐ REPORT OF FEDERAL ACTION	2. APPLICANT'S APPLICATION	a. NUMBER		3. STATE APPLICATION IDENTIFIER	a. NUMBER	
			b. DATE _Year month day_ 19			b. DATE ASSIGNED _Year month day_ 19	

4. LEGAL APPLICANT/RECIPIENT

a. Applicant Name :
b. Organization Unit :
c. Street/P.O. Box :
d. City :   e. County :
f. State :   g. ZIP Code:
h. Contact Person (Name & telephone No.) :

5. FEDERAL EMPLOYER IDENTIFICATION NO.

6. PROGRAM (From Federal Catalog)
a. NUMBER ☐☐ ● ☐☐☐
b. TITLE

7. TITLE AND DESCRIPTION OF APPLICANT'S PROJECT

8. TYPE OF APPLICANT/RECIPIENT
A—State
B—Interstate
C—Substate District
D—County
E—City
F—School District
G—Special Purpose District
H—Community Action Agency
I—Higher Educational Institution
J—Indian Tribe
K—Other (Specify):
Enter appropriate letter ☐

9. TYPE OF ASSISTANCE
A—Basic Grant
B—Supplemental Grant
C—Loan
D—Insurance
E—Other
Enter appropriate letter(s) ☐

10. AREA OF PROJECT IMPACT (Names of cities, counties, States, etc.)

11. ESTIMATED NUMBER OF PERSONS BENEFITING

12. TYPE OF APPLICATION
A—New   C—Revision   E—Augmentation
B—Renewal   D—Continuation
Enter appropriate letter ☐

13. PROPOSED FUNDING		14. CONGRESSIONAL DISTRICTS OF:		15. TYPE OF CHANGE (For 12c or 12e)
a. FEDERAL	$ .00	a. APPLICANT	b. PROJECT	A—Increase Dollars F—Other (Specify):
b. APPLICANT	.00			B—Decrease Dollars
c. STATE	.00	16. PROJECT START DATE _Year month day_ 19	17. PROJECT DURATION _Months_	C—Increase Duration D—Decrease Duration E—Cancellation
d. LOCAL	.00			_Enter appropriate letter(s)_ ☐☐
e. OTHER	.00	18. ESTIMATED DATE TO BE SUBMITTED TO FEDERAL AGENCY ▶ _Year month day_ 19		19. EXISTING FEDERAL IDENTIFICATION NUMBER
f. TOTAL	$ .00			

20. FEDERAL AGENCY TO RECEIVE REQUEST (Name, City, State, ZIP code)	21. REMARKS ADDED ☐ Yes ☐ No

22. THE APPLICANT CERTIFIES THAT ▶	a. To the best of my knowledge and belief, data in this preapplication/application are true and correct, the document has been duly authorized by the governing body of the applicant and the applicant will comply with the attached assurances if the assistance is approved.	b. If required by OMB Circular A-95 this application was submitted, pursuant to instructions therein, to appropriate clearinghouses and all responses are attached: (1) (2) (3)	No response	Response attached
			☐ ☐ ☐	☐ ☐ ☐

23. CERTIFYING REPRESENTATIVE	a. TYPED NAME AND TITLE	b. SIGNATURE	c. DATE SIGNED _Year month day_ 19

24. AGENCY NAME		25. APPLICATION RECEIVED _Year month day_ 19
26. ORGANIZATIONAL UNIT	27. ADMINISTRATIVE OFFICE	28. FEDERAL APPLICATION IDENTIFICATION
29. ADDRESS		30. FEDERAL GRANT IDENTIFICATION

31. ACTION TAKEN	32. FUNDING		_Year month day_	34. STARTING DATE _Year month day_ 19
☐ a. AWARDED	a. FEDERAL	$ .00	33. ACTION DATE ▶ 19	
☐ b. REJECTED	b. APPLICANT	.00	35. CONTACT FOR ADDITIONAL INFORMATION (Name and telephone number)	36. ENDING DATE _Year month day_ 19
☐ c. RETURNED FOR AMENDMENT	c. STATE	.00		
☐ d. DEFERRED	d. LOCAL	.00		37. REMARKS ADDED
☐ e. WITHDRAWN	e. OTHER	.00		☐ Yes ☐ No
	f. TOTAL	$ .00		

38. FEDERAL AGENCY A-95 ACTION	a. In taking above action, any comments received from clearinghouses were considered. If agency response is due under provisions of Part 1, OMB Circular A-95, it has been or is being made.	b. FEDERAL AGENCY A-95 OFFICIAL (Name and telephone no.)

SECTION I—APPLICANT/RECIPIENT DATA
SECTION II—CERTIFICATION
SECTION III—FEDERAL AGENCY ACTION

Figure 3. Federal agency application form.

For proposals to government funding agencies that provide forms as part of their application material, a title page is not necessary. Figure 3 is an example of the kind of information required by some federal agencies as part of their application kit. This example is Standard Form 424, which is required in all federal intergovernmental programs. In effect this form represents a title page. Detailed program and financial information to elaborate on each item is presented on additional forms that are provided and must be used in order for the proposal to be considered.

It is also important to pay attention to the length of the title. Avoid long complex titles and those that contain highly technical language since you do not know how sophisticated the reader may be in the technical area covered by the proposal. The exceptions to this are many research proposals, particularly in the sciences and the biomedical field. Some federal funders limit the number of letters that may appear in the title, and one should adhere to these restrictions.

HEADINGS AND TABLE OF CONTENTS AND THEIR IMPORTANCE

Effective communication between the proposal writer and the reviewer requires that there be congruence between what one writes and what the other person perceives has been said. Research has shown that this congruence is difficult to attain but that various techniques can help improve the communication process. One of these techniques is the use of headings and subheadings. Headings are so effective because they tell the reader what is going to be presented before the person starts reading. This cues the reader's perception of the material. For example, when you start to read this paragraph, the heading "Headings and Table of Contents and Their Importance," cues you to expect and look for a particular kind of information. Headings reduce the extent to which the reader may perceive that something else is being discussed. In addition, the use of headings provides a break in the narrative and gives the reader a "rest" from going from paragraph to paragraph of straight unbroken text. Finally, headings convey to the reader a sense of organization of the material that may not occur if there is a long unbroken narrative presentation.

The best way to integrate headings into the proposal is to use one of the standard outline formats. The most typical format uses a Roman numeral for each major section, a capital letter for each subsection, an Arabic numeral for each section under the subsection, and a lowercase letter for each heading under the numeral. An example of this format follows:

IV. Program Description
    A. General Approach
    B. Identification and Recruitment of Participants
        1. Characteristics of High-Risk Persons
        2. Eligibility for Service
        3. Recruitment Methods
    C. Counseling Programs
        1. Individual Counseling
            a. Youths
            b. Families
        2. Group Counseling
            a. Youth Groups
            b. Parent Groups

Some proposal writers and some government funders prefer the use of a sequential numbering system as an alternative format to designate and refer to the various sections of the proposal. Using the same outline, this system looks like this:

4. Program Description
    4.1 General Approach
    4.2 Identification and Recruitment of Participants
        4.2.1 Characteristics of High-Risk Persons
        4.2.2 Eligibility for Service
        4.2.3. Recruitment Methods
    4.3. Counseling Programs
        4.3.1 Individual Counseling
            4.3.1.1. Youths
            4.3.1.2. Families
        4.3.2 Group Counseling
            4.3.2.1 Youth Groups
            4.3.2.2. Parent Groups

Each heading should describe the narrative material that follows the heading. It should convey the essence of the material and represent the central idea, concept, or theme that is the core of that particular section.

TABLE OF CONTENTS

The headings used throughout the narrative proposal are repeated in the table of contents with the addition of the page number on which each heading appears. Thus, the table of contents for the example given above would appear as follows:

Table of Contents

			Page
IV.	Program Description		9
	A.	General Approach	9
	B.	Identification and Recruitment of Participants	10
		1. Characteristics of High-Risk Persons	10
		2. Eligibility for Service	11
		3. Recruitment Methods	11
	C.	Counseling Programs	12
		1. Individual Counseling	12
		a. Youths	13
		b. Families	14
		2. Group Counseling	15
		a. Youth Groups	16
		b. Parent Groups	18

The entire table of contents should always have a heading of its own at the top of the page: Table of Contents. The table of contents presents the reader with an overall picture of the major topics covered in the proposal. When carefully devised headings are used, they instill a sense of unity and coherence to the proposal. In many ways the headings and the table of contents can be thought of as the headlines that tell what the story is going to be about, in the same way that newspaper headlines and subheadings are used.

A frequent error made by proposal writers is that they pay too little attention to the use of headings and the wording of the headings when they are used. They tend to regard headings as a relatively unimportant aspect of the proposal. Nothing could be further from the truth since this element of the proposal is a major contributor to its impact and indicates how well organized the applicant appears to be to the funder.

SUMMARY

A summary or abstract of the proposal should be included if the proposal exceeds six to eight pages, as many proposals do. The summary should briefly cover the highlights of the material in each section of the proposal. One way to help structure the summary is to allocate a paragraph to each major section of the proposal. This will generally result in a one- to two-page summary. At times, the letter of transmittal may include an adequate summary, but for longer proposals it is necessary to have a separate one.

Some government funding agencies include a box on the first page of their application forms to be used for the summary. They often prescribe the number of words or space that can be used. One form states "500 words or less," another states "a single spaced abstract not to exceed 30 lines." Some federal funders and foundations may prepare their own summary of the proposal for their reviewers. Preparing your own summary allows you to stress the points you want to emphasize.

In addition to covering all of the major points in the proposal, a good summary includes a brief statement explaining how the proposal is responsive to the funder's requirements and interests. Many proposal writers also include budget request information in the summary. This may not be advisable, however, since some funders want to review the substance of the proposal separate from the financial information.

One of the errors made in preparing summaries is merely selecting certain sentences from the body of the narrative and placing them in the summary. This inevitably results in an awkward and disjointed summary. Another error is to write the summary in a way that makes it seem alien and inconsistent with the rest of the proposal. The best summary is one that captures the essence of the proposal, impresses the funder with its clarity, and makes the reader want to read the whole story.

Summaries take a good deal of time to prepare since it is often harder to explain something briefly than at great length.

In the words of one funder, "The summary should provide readers with the following information: who will do what, to whom, how, when, where." In addition, the summary should impart a sense of the project's expected outcomes, accomplishments, or benefits.

Sometimes when an organization is exploring funding possibilities, a summary of from two to four pages is prepared as a prospectus. This may be sent to a variety of funders, usually foundations, to ascertain their interest in the project. It is always desirable to check with the funding source to see if the funder is willing to review such a prospectus. Summaries of this type resemble mini-proposals or letter proposals, which are discussed in detail in chapter 5. Some funders only want to receive short letter proposals. In such cases the construction of the short proposal differs somewhat from that of a summary, as explained in chapter 5.

INTRODUCTION

The introduction to the proposal establishes both the writing style for the proposal as well as its central theme. The introduction is the first substantive section of the proposal and is often simply titled, "Introduction." It should include the following:

- The title, with a short description of the proposed program
- The name of the applicant organization and the funding source
- The RFP, RFA, program, or interest of the funder to which the proposal responds
- The geographic area where the program will take place
- A description of the kind of persons who will be served and, if possible, how many will be served
- Why the program is significant and its overall purpose
- The basic programmatic concept or approach and the major kind of activity that will be undertaken

The introduction should heighten the reader's curiosity and interest so that the reader wants to continue reading. To this end, the introduction must be clear and straightforward; the explanation of complex ideas should be left for later sections of the proposal. After the proposal is completed, it may be necessary to revise the introduction to eliminate any ambiguities or fuzziness that might have crept in during its initial drafting. All good proposal writers find, as they proceed with the proposal, that they must go back and revise former sections. Revising is a sign of good writing and one should not hesitate to make multiple revisions.

The introductory section of the proposal can also be used to describe the applying organization and enhance its credibility. Some proposal writers believe that the introduction should be used mainly for this purpose. However, an overly long description of the organization can be distracting to the reader who wants to get to the substance of the proposal. It is better to include a brief description of the applying organization in the introduction and to include more detail elsewhere in the proposal. For example, a capability statement, as described later in this chapter, can be attached to the proposal.

It is important to establish the central idea, theme, or organizing principle that guides the proposed program in the introduction. This theme usually represents a combination of a definition of the problem that the proposal addresses and the particular programmatic approach that will be used. This theme can then be further defined, clarified, and expanded upon in subsequent sections of the proposal devoted to defining the problem and describing the proposed program activities.

The introduction should include a brief description of the nature, scope, and significance of the problem. Similarly, a general statement of the program methods should be given in the introduction to prepare the reader for the detailed program description that will come later in the proposal.

Writing the introduction can be difficult. The temptation is to want to say everything at once since the proposal writer knows the importance of fully describing the problem, how all of the elements of the proposed program are interrelated, and how they will impact the problem. To avoid falling prey to this temptation you must say to yourself, "I can't say everything here." Be content to pick out one or two major aspects of the problem and of the program to include in the introduction. Usually, no one will know the difference but you.

Each section of the proposal should set the framework or context for the section that follows. This is accomplished by the logical flow of the material and by the use of bridging sentences at the end of each section. For example, the introduction may end with the sentence, "The next section of the proposal describes the specific purpose and objectives of the project."

PURPOSE AND OBJECTIVES

A statement of the overall purpose or goal(s) of the project and a listing of its specific objectives are crucial to presenting a strong, clear proposal. The statement of purpose and objectives may be included as a part or subsection of the introduction or presented as a separate section with its own heading, "Purpose and Objectives." Both the substance of this part of the proposal as well as its format are important factors in preparing a high-quality proposal.

There is quite a bit of confusion over the words used to indicate what belongs in this part of the proposal. For example, what is being referred to here as objectives may be referred to as "specific aims" by many government funders. What we are calling purposes may be called "goals." Others may refer to what we are calling objectives as "goals." Regardless of the nomenclature used, the principles and methods presented below will assure the clarity of the proposal and will be consistent with the intent of the funder in asking for this material. The key to understanding how to present this part of the proposal is to be able to distinguish between the various levels of specificity regarding what the project is intended to accomplish.

The purpose represents the broad goal(s) of the program and can generally be stated in one or two sentences or short paragraphs. The most frequent error made in stating a purpose is to discuss the purpose's means rather than to focus on its desired achievements, which are expressed in the way of outcomes or benefits. For example, it is not sufficient to state a purpose as "to provide a drug abuse prevention program" or "to establish a neighborhood health center." Rather, the purpose should be stated as "to reduce the incidence of drug and alcohol use," or "to improve the level of individual, family, and community health." It is not a purpose "to hold a conference on teen pregnancy." Rather, the purpose might be "to increase understanding of the factors that contribute to teen pregnancy." In each of the examples given above the distinction is made between an activity (e.g., holding a conference) and an outcome (e.g., increasing understanding). Sometimes, a program may have more than one purpose. For example, "to reduce the incidence of drug and alcohol use and increase the availability of treatment services. "Also when stating the purpose, one can go on to state what the major activity will be: "To improve the level of individual, family, and community health by establishing a neighborhood health center that is accessible to low-income individuals."

The objectives, on the other hand, should be written as more specific statements of what will be accomplished. From the standpoint of format, the objectives are best presented in list form rather than paragraph form. To help identify them, the objectives may be numbered, for example:

The specific objectives are:

1. ——————————————————
2. ——————————————————
3. ——————————————————
4. ——————————————————

Most proposals seem to require between three and seven objectives, although it is not possible to prescribe a set number. The objectives are, in effect, a list of the specific accomplishments that the program will achieve. As such, the objectives can be thought of as the program's resulting benefits to individuals, families, groups, communities, organizations, society, or a field of knowledge or practice. From the standpoint of the funder, the objectives represent social, economic, political, physical, cultural, or scientific achievements that will be realized as a result of the grant. Thus, the objectives should be stated in specific terms, should be significant, should be attainable, and should be stated in way that makes it possible to determine the extent to which they might be achieved.

Objectives stand halfway between the general statement of purpose and the detailed explanation of the program activities that will be furnished later in the proposal. The objectives represent a strategy to reach a particular purpose or goal. The program, in this sense, represents the tactics or methods that will be employed.

The benefits that are expressed in objectives usually have intrinsic value; that is, they tend to be well accepted as being worthwhile in their own right. For example, the objectives of a program to improve the social and cultural well-being of older people might be to:

1. Reduce social isolation
2. Increase ability to cope with life changes
3. Facilitate being part of a larger community
4. Increase contact with other persons
5. Increase the availability of plays and concerts

All of these are benefits that are generally accepted as being desirable. Therefore, one usually does not need to justify the *value* of objectives. It is necessary, however, to justify the *need* for having each objective, and this is done in a subsequent section of the proposal called Problem Definition and Need (or Significance in the case of research proposals).

Objectives should be expressed using words that explicitly indicate both action and a measurable result. Use active verbs such as reduce, increase, improve, decrease, make more accessible, identify, recruit, demonstrate, formulate, and similar verbs.

The following are some additional examples of how to formulate objectives. In the case of a project of counseling and group activities for single-parent families, the overall purpose might be to "strengthen family life." The objectives for this program might be:

1. To increase meaningful relationships among families with similar problems
2. To reduce isolation among single-parent families
3. To improve child-rearing skills

4. To facilitate the ability of families to identify the source of problems that concerns them
5. To improve the ways in which families make decisions and allocate roles

Examples of objectives related to a neighborhood health center whose purpose is the "improvement of individual, family, and community health" might include:

1. To make preventive and primary care more accessible
2. To decrease the incidence of morbidity and mortality
3. To reduce environmental health hazards
4. To provide for continuity of care through the coordination of necessary health services
5. To reduce the extent to which hospitalization is required

In all of these examples the objectives are expressed in specific, active, outcome-oriented terms. Other terms such as "help families," "educate families," "attack health problems," even though they use active verbs, are undesirable because they do not convey a sense of what will actually be accomplished.

The program methods (i.e., what will be done) should not be confused with program objectives (i.e., the results or the ends of the program).

The methods by which the program will carry out each objective should be described in a later section of the proposal on program activities.

Proposal writers need to push themselves to define outcomes as specifically as possible. For example, an objective, "to improve the skills of reading teachers" can be strengthened by defining the kinds of skills that will be improved. This objective would then be stated, "to improve the diagnostic and remedial skills of reading teachers." Similarly, specificity regarding the characteristics of the populations to be served adds to effectiveness of the statement of objectives. For example, the objective "to raise the reading levels of children" can be improved by stating "to raise the reading levels of children in public school grades one through four."

Many proposal writers and program planners believe that objectives should always be stated in terms of an observable and measurable behavior. In all of the examples of objectives given above the outcomes can be behaviorally measured. For example, "to improve child rearing skills" can be measured by developing a list of such skills and then measuring the extent to which the participants in the program learned these skills. Thus, the objectives can provide the basis for designing the evaluation of the program since they are the criteria upon which effectiveness can be determined. The design of the evaluation section of the proposal is discussed later in this chapter.

Whereas behavioral objectives are appropriate for program and training proposals, they may not work as well for research proposals, in which the outcomes are expressed in specific kinds of information, findings, conclusions, and reports resulting from the research. But even in the case of research proposals, the objectives can be made more attractive by stating them in outcome-oriented active terms. For example, it is better to state an objective for a study of hospitals as "to determine the extent to which hospital beds are utilized" than to state the objective as "to study the utilization of hospital beds." The first statement specifies that there will be a specific expected outcome, that is, a determination of the extent to which beds are utilized. Chapter 6 discusses this aspect of research proposals in detail.

The objectives provide the framework for the organization of the problem definition and need section of the proposal, in which the problem and need are described and analyzed. If, for example, one objective in a program to strengthen family life is "to reduce social isolation of the families that come for service," then the need section should discuss the nature and extent of social isolation among the families to be served and how isolation contributes to the weakening of the family and the occurrence of family problems. Similarly, the objectives set the framework for the section of the proposal on program description and activities. In the example just cited, one must be sure to include activities that are clearly focused on decreasing social isolation, such as organizing support groups among the families to be served, providing transportation services, and the like.

In some governmental funding programs the major objectives (or goals) are predetermined by the funding agency and set forth in the program announcement, RFP, or RFA. Funder stated objectives (or other material) should never be used in a proposal without proper reference. Otherwise, it might imply that the material originated with the applicant.

Usually, funders state rather broad objectives and the burden is on the applicant to make them more specific. For example, an RFA from the Federal Office for Substance Abuse Prevention indicates that the "goals" of one of its program announcements are to:

- Increase the availability and accessibility of prevention, early intervention, and treatment services
- Improve birth outcomes of women who used alcohol and other drugs during pregnancy
- Reduce the severity of impairment among children born to substance-using women

In such a case, the job of the applicant is to make these general objectives more specific by developing subobjectives for each of the broader ones. When funders prescribe objectives it can be assumed that a major requirement for the proposal is to include a well-defined set of activities and methods showing exactly how each of the prescribed objectives will be implemented. In addition, because of the confusion over terminology, some funders may ask for a statement of subobjectives for each major objective. Usually, what is meant by subobjective is a statement of an activity. For example, a subobjective for an objective such as "increase public awareness," might be "prepare ten public-service announcements."

In other cases the application material may be vague. For example, the application guidelines for one program state: "the purpose of this program is the creation of a broad artistic climate in the United States in which its indigenous musical arts will thrive with distinction through artistic, educational and archival programs." In this type of situation the proposal writers must develop their own specific objectives.

Some proposal writers suggest quantifying objectives whenever possible with statements such as "to reduce high school truancy by 30 percent." This practice is sometimes required by funders and is appropriate to some projects. However, it often is unrealistic and does not reflect the reality of the state of the art in the social and behavioral field.

PROBLEM DEFINITION AND NEED

The problem definition and need section of the proposal should explain and document the nature and extent of the problem that has resulted in a need for the proposed program. Convincing reasons should be given using available evidence and logical argument to establish the need for the program. This section of the proposal gives the applicant the opportunity to demonstrate a thorough understanding and familiarity with the field in which the proposed program will operate. Thus, in addition to establishing the need for the program, per se, this section has the added impact of establishing the credibility of the applicant.

SCOPE OF THE PROBLEM

In presenting the need for the program one should be careful not to oversell the scope of the problem but to focus on its immediate limited aspects that the proposal will address. For example, the proposal may be for a new program in a mental health clinic to provide services to women who have been abused. While the explanation of the problem might include a description of the extent of abuse and domestic violence in the country, it should concentrate on the specific manifestations of this problem in the area the program will operate and on the specific group of women that the program will serve.

CAUSAL EXPLANATIONS

One of the issues that must be decided is how far to go in presenting an explanation of the *causes* of the problem and where to place such material in the proposal. Depending on the flow of the entire proposal, information on the cause of the problem may be a brief part of the introduction, may be in the needs section, may be a separate section presenting the frame of reference or rationale for the project (as described in the next part of this chapter), or, sometimes can be located in the beginning of the activities section of the proposal. Assuming that it comes in the needs section, it should be presented early in the section and should, if possible, include documentation from the literature.

If the definition of the nature of the problem and its causes differs from the usually accepted definitions, explain specifically in what ways the definition is different. As an example, assume that the proposal is directed toward preventing juvenile delinquency and rests upon the idea that delinquency is in large part the result of unresponsive social institutions such as the schools and the employment market. Two things should be done in the proposal: (1) The proposal should explain exactly how the schools and the employment market contribute to the problem, and (2) the proposal should recognize other causal explanations of the primary factors contributing to delinquency, such as the family and the lack of adequate role models, and then explain why these factors are not being focused on in the proposed program. One can then go on to show how the school-employment market explanation leads to the particular program strategy, objectives, and activities that are being proposed. This establishes the overall conceptual framework, for the proposal, as well as for the premises and assumptions upon which the proposal is based. For this reason, it is desirable to present this material early in the proposal so that the reader will be able to place the other proposal material in the proper context.

DOCUMENTING NEED

The major content for most needs sections will be the documentation of the need for the program. There are four main ways to convincingly document need, as follows:

- Quantitative Documentation
- Qualitative Documentation
- Documentation of the Limitations of Existing Programs
- Documentation of the Evidence of Demand

QUANTITATIVE DOCUMENTATION. Quantitative documentation refers to the use of statistical and other quantitative information to describe and analyze the need for the proposed activity. The main focus here is to identify the population to be served, its size and demographic characteristics, the incidence and prevalence of the relevant social, economic, or other problems among this population, the distribution of relevant risk factors (if any), and other pertinent information regarding its characteristics that might help to establish the need for the proposed activities.

In presenting quantitative information it is important to avoid certain mistakes that are often made. One of these is to assume that the "facts speak for themselves." Nothing could be further from the truth. Demographic and other quantitative data are always subject to interpretation, and different readers give different meanings to the same information. Therefore, always point out the significance of the data that are being presented. For example, information regarding the number and percentage of persons living below the poverty line may be given as follows: "There are twenty thousand persons living below the poverty line in the community and this comprises 28 percent of the population." To the reader the information is meaningless unless some significance can be attached to the figures. Is this a lot? Is it more than other communities? Is the number going up or down?

The data in this example can be given added meaning through the use of comparison and contrast. Thus, one may add statements such as: "This is the fourth highest rate among the thirty-three counties in the state." Or, "This is an increase of forty-five hundred persons or 30 percent from the prior year."

Another common mistake is overloading the reader with either too much data or presenting very complex data. The solution to this problem is to avoid trying to say everything at once because you understand that there are all sorts of interconnections and subtleties involved. This is done by breaking down information into as simple pieces as possible and then presenting the various pieces of information in separate sentences or individual tables. Another effective method in presenting quantitative documentation is to use one or two bar charts, pie charts, or line graphs.

Whenever tables and charts are used they should be numbered; refer to them in the text by using phrases such as "Table 1 indicates . . ." or "as shown in Figure 1. . . ." In addition to having a number, each table and chart should also have a descriptive title that explains the content of the material being presented.

Some of the sources of quantitative data include surveys and studies, U.S government census reports and population surveys, the U.S. government *Statistical Abstract*, reports of state and local planning agencies, reports of legislative committees, and reports of federal, state, and local task forces and commissions.

QUALITATIVE DOCUMENTATION. Qualitative documentation refers to the use of statements that make a logical connection between different factors or ideas that explain the need for the proposed activities. Examples of such statements supporting the need for a family life education program might be: "Family life is weakened by a lack of communication among family members. As a consequence each member of the family may have many misconceptions about other members that can lead to unexpressed anger and unnecessary conflict."

Statements such as these can be expanded and bolstered with very brief examples. When qualitative arguments are presented they can be further strengthened by citing references from the literature, research findings, and empirical evidence. Quantitative and qualitative material need not be presented separately. Often, the most convincing need argument can be made by weaving together qualitative and quantitative information.

Also keep in mind that the material defining the nature of the problem and its causes that may have been presented earlier in this section of the proposal also contributes to the strength of the qualitative aspects of documenting the need.

DOCUMENTATION OF THE LIMITATIONS OF EXISTING PROGRAMS. In the case of most program proposals, there are most likely one or more programs in the community operating in the same field as the program being proposed. It is important to recognize these other programs in the proposal and to show how the existing programs do not meet the needs by pointing out their limitations. The proposal should also stress how the proposed program differs from the existing programs. Often there may be various studies or reports that can be referenced to document the limitation of existing programs. Other sources to use for this purpose include newspaper stories and, in some cases, the annual reports of the other agencies may include information regarding their inability to meet certain needs because of financial limitations, staff shortages, and the like. Another technique for presenting material related to other programs is to show how the proposed program builds upon prior efforts of your own or other organizations.

In the case of research proposals, it is always necessary to refer to prior research in the same field and to show how the proposed research is related to prior work. This may involve overcoming the limitations of that work, extending the prior research, or by further validating or testing the results of other research. Similar approaches can be used in making reference to prior program or training efforts in the case of proposals in these fields.

DOCUMENTATION OF THE EVIDENCE OF DEMAND. Another way to document need is to furnish evidence of a demand for the program. Waiting lists, surveys of participants, lists of potential participants, and results of community meetings can be used for this purpose. Also, statements from other agencies, government officials, and recognized community leaders can be included in this section of the proposal or referred to and attached as supporting documents to provide evidence of demand. Similarly, newspaper stories showing concern for the problem addressed by the proposal and a demand for the proposed program may be referred to and attached to the proposal.

Sometimes it is desirable to conduct a special survey of people to document the need and demand for the program. In addition, one might hold a meeting or series of meetings of interested people to discuss the need for the proposed program and the problem it addresses. Newspaper articles about such meetings or surveys can be prepared for the local press and, when published, can be referred to and attached to the proposal.

ORGANIZING THE NEEDS SECTION

The needs section should begin with an introductory subsection that includes a brief general description of the problem and of the causal definition being used, if any. The introductory part should also tell the reader what will follow, for example, "This section of the proposal describes the scope of the need for daycare, problems related to the quality of care, the lack of up-to-date information on daycare practices among daycare workers, the need to provide parents with better information on good daycare services, and the need to strengthen the relationship between daycare centers and the public schools." This kind of statement focuses the reader's attention on the material you want to stress by cueing him or her to perceive the material that follows according to your emphasis. Headings and subheadings, as pointed out earlier, further focus the reader's attention.

An effective way to organize the material in the needs section is to use the proposal's objectives as the framework. In a sense, the problem and need represent the negative state of the objectives. For example, one objective might be "to improve the quality of daycare by distributing up-to-date information on child development and daycare methods." In such a case, the needs section should include a subsection headed "Quality of Care Problems." Information can then be presented to document the reasons for poor quality of care offered by daycare centers, such as the lack of qualified staff and the absence of sufficient training among daycare workers. There could also be another section that shows how there is a lack of up-to-date information among daycare workers, which could be provided through in-service training and by bringing in experts in the field. The subsection could also include an indication of the demand for such information by presenting the results of a survey of daycare centers as well as by presenting letters from center directors indicating that they believe the information is needed and that they are willing to cooperate with the proposed program. Similar subsections of the needs section should be prepared which relate to each of the other objectives included in the proposal.

FRAME OF REFERENCE OR RATIONALE

The rationale for the proposed program may be included in the introduction, the needs section, the program activities section, or in a separate section. The frame of reference or rationale covers the philosophy or perspective that guides the proposal. It is usually an abstract conceptual statement that conveys to the funder the thoughts, ideas, concepts, assumptions, and beliefs guiding the proposal. In many cases this rationale may correspond to the problem definition material set forth at the beginning of the needs section. It may also correspond to the material presented in explaining the program activities. In the case of research proposals, usually a separate section is devoted to explaining the conceptual framework that guides the research design. This aspect of research proposals is discussed further in chapter 6.

A part of the frame of reference/rationale can include what is referred to as state-of-the-art information. This is a synopsis of similar or related work done in the field covered by the proposal and may include a criticism of the existing program methods. Preparation of this information requires considerable research since it is usually based on a review of the relevant literature. When material based on the literature is presented, it should always include the proper citations and footnotes. State-of-the-art information in program proposals focuses mainly on methodology, that is, what is known about the manner in which programs are organized and what is known about the efficacy of various program methods used to achieve objectives similar to those sought in the proposed program. This material answers questions such as, "what do we know about the way to help people recover from alcoholism?" "what approaches work best to prevent rehospitalization of former mental patients?" "what techniques result in creating greater awareness of environmental hazards in suburban communities?"

Taken together, the objectives, problem definition, need, and rationale provide the legitimation and justification for the program activities for which support is being requested. These activities should be fully explained in the next section of the proposal as discussed below.

DESCRIPTION OF PROGRAM ACTIVITIES

The description of program activities is the longest section of the proposal and should describe in detail each activity that will be undertaken and how each activity will be carried out. Every major activity or task should be included with a description of the methods and procedures that will be employed to carry out the activity.

This section of the proposal may be referred to by a variety of titles including, "Activities," "Program," "Program Activities," "Methods," "Implementation Plan," "Project Implementation," "Work Plan," "Action Plan," "Program Plan," "Approach," "Operations," or some other descriptive phrase.

Two major requirements stand out in relation to preparing this section of the proposal. First is the need for specificity regarding *what* will be done and *how* it will be done. Second is the need to show that the program activities will implement the program's objectives as presented earlier in the proposal. The objectives are the end results or achievements the program seeks; the activities are the ways, means, or methods by which the objectives will be realized. To the funder, this section of the proposal represents the concrete work that is being funded. And, in addition to being the key description of the proposed program, it is also a way to judge the applicant's familiarity with the field and the applicant's competence to perform the proposed work.

ORGANIZING THE PROGRAM ACTIVITIES SECTION

Most programs include many different activities and each should be described. From the format standpoint, the most effective way to present the program description material is to group similar activities together. For example, if it is a new program for which a number of start-up activities are necessary such as locating a facility, forming a board or committee, or recruiting staff and training staff, these activities can all be shown as a subsection under a heading such as "Preparatory Activities." Similarly, if a variety of educational programs such as forums, classes, and movies will be offered, these can all be grouped under a heading "Educational Activities." When activities are grouped in this way, it is essential to list and describe each specific activity under its appropriate subheading.

When the activities section is organized in this manner, it is usually possible to present the activities and the tasks or steps in a sequential manner. A partial example of the grouped activities format is shown below.

A. Planning and Preparatory Activities
   1. Recruiting Staff
   2. Training Staff
   3. Selecting Advisory Committee
   4. Obtaining and Equipping Offices
B. Educational Programs
   1. Preparation of Drug Abuse Manual
      a. Obtaining Material
      b. Production of Manual
      c. Distribution of Manual
   2. Organization and Implementation of Drug Abuse Workshops
      a. Selection of Workshop Leaders
      b. Selection of Workshop Participants
      c. Organization of the Workshop
      d. Workshop Content
      e. Conduct of Workshops
      f. Workshop Format and Schedule
C. Counseling Program
   1. Intake Procedures
   2. Counseling Approaches
      a. Individual Counseling
      b. Peer Group Counseling

DESCRIBING THE ACTIVITIES

There should be a full description of the activity under each of the headings and subheadings, including specific methods to be used, how the activity will be organized, and the characteristics and number of people to be served.

One of the frequent weaknesses in presenting this section of a proposal is the tendency to describe only *what* will be done, but not to describe *how* it will be done. For example, in proposing a mental health service, one of the activities may be listed as "intake" and the proposal may explain that there will be an intake unit to screen prospective applicants for service. This is a description of *what* will be done. The proposal is strengthened by describing *how* the screening will be carried out. This can be achieved by listing the criteria that will be used to determine eligibility, the manner in which the criteria will be used, the way in which the intake activities will be staffed, the efforts that will be made to explain the intake process to applicants, and the methods whereby people in the community will be made aware of the availability of the service.

In addition to explaining how each activity will be carried out, it is desirable, wherever possible, to provide estimates of how many people will be served by each activity. Also, the characteristics of the people to be served can be described, such as age, sex, and problems presented.

For some proposals it can be effective to list each of the objectives and then to describe under the objective each implementing program activity. For example, in the case of a drug abuse prevention program, the format might look as follows:

Objective A: To increase the availability of reliable information on the effects of the use of hard drugs to high-school students. Activities to implement this objective would include:

1. Preparing a drug-information manual

2. Scheduling and carrying out discussion groups for all high-school students

3. Training a group of high-school students to serve as peer educational counselors

In using this format one must be sure to then go on to describe how each of these implementing activities would be organized and carried out. For instance, under "Preparing a drug-information manual" each step or task involved should be described, including:

a. the kind of information that would be included
b. the way in which the decision would be made regarding the information to be includedz:
c. the sources from which the information would be obtained
d. the methods by which the information would be obtained
e. the steps that would be taken in actual writing and producing the manual
f. the description of the manual's format
g. the manner in which the manual would be distributed and used

Objectives	Activities			
	Counseling	Education	Health Services	Referral
Reduction of Truancy	X	X		
Improved Peer Relationships		X		X
Increased Understanding of Drug Abuse		X	X	

Figure 4. Sample activities chart.

The foregoing format may not lend itself to proposals in which the same activity is an implementing device for more than one objective. However, the same kind of step-by-step description of the activity should be used.

Another way of relating specific activities to objectives is by using a simple chart, listing each objective on one axis and each major group of activities on the other axis. Wherever an activity directly implements an objective, a check is placed in the appropriate space or box. An example of such a chart is shown above in Figure 4.

In the final analysis, the program activities are what the funder is really supporting; so they should be complete, specific, and task-oriented. If it has not been established in other parts of the proposal, this section of the proposal can also contain information on the reasons why particular program methods have been chosen and why these appear to be viable and effective. At the same time, reference can be made to any available evidence of effectiveness of similar program techniques. Also, the choice of certain methods can be linked to the particular characteristics or needs of those to be served. Some of the limitations of other methods may be discussed.

In addition to the narrative description of the proposed activities, it is also helpful to use charts to show the organization of activities and/or the flow of people through the program. An example of a flowchart is shown in Figure 5.

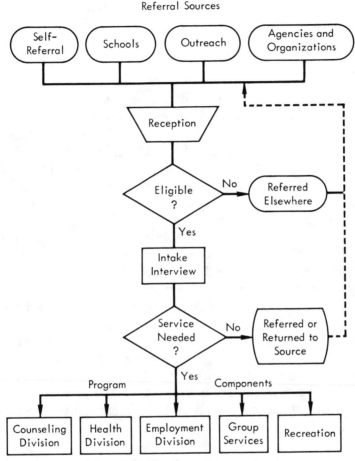

Referral Sources

Figure 5. Sample flowchart.

FUTURE PLANS AND FINANCING

More and more funders are raising the question of future plans for programs initiated with special funds. These plans should be explained somewhere in the proposal—either in the activities section, in a separate section, in the letter of transmittal, or in the introduction. If the program will generate its own support through fees and contributions, this should be indicated. If after initial funding for one to three years it will become part of a larger ongoing operation, or if it will then be supported by another source, the plan for bringing this about should be specifically described.

FACILITIES

A description of physical facilities and program equipment should be included, especially when proposed programs require special facilities or when a considerable part of the requested budget is needed for physical facilities or equipment. For example, if the proposed program includes a set of activities requiring the use of portable videotape equipment, the proposal should list each piece of the necessary equipment and explain the reason for the selection of this particular type of equipment and its programmatic advantages. Similarly, a program for an emergency shelter for abused women should include a description of the location and kind of facility that would be used and its programmatic advantages. An explanation of the costs associated with these items should appear in the budget section of the proposal.

Many foundations and government funders will not support the purchase of major equipment or other capital expenditures. Some corporations and foundations do put a considerable portion of their resources into physical facilities and will provide you with an outline of what they require for capital projects.

ORGANIZATIONAL STRUCTURE, ADMINISTRATION, AND STAFFING

ORGANIZATION AND MANAGEMENT

Boards and committees should be described in terms of their membership, composition, and responsibilities. The manner in which they are appointed and their relationship to each other should also be pointed out.

Several other aspects of the organizational plan should also be explained. These include the locus for policy and program decision making, the hierarchy of personnel, lines of communication, and arrangements to assure direction, coordination, control, and accountability of the project.

If the proposed program is part of a larger operation, an explanation is needed of the way in which the proposed program fits into the overall structure. If formal working relationships with other agencies are required, these linkages should be described.

Charts can be used to help clarify the organizational plan. A sample of a typical organizational chart is shown in Figure 6. This chart combines both administrative units (i.e., boards and committees) and staff organization. It is also possible to use two charts: one showing administrative units, the other only the staff organization. The charts must be titled appropriately and be referred to in the text.

The organizational chart should be accompanied by a narrative that describes:

1. The board of directors, the size of the board, the persons on the board and the organizations that they represent, and the responsibilities of the board for policy making, fund raising, selection of personnel, establishment of personnel policies, and monitoring of the program.

2. The role, function, and responsibilities of any committees shown on the chart.

3. The delineation of the responsibilities of the executive director including administrative duties, relationship with the board and board committees, and responsibilities for selection and supervision of the remainder of the staff.

4. The description of the management responsibilities of any top staff such as associate directors, and the directors of major units. If these persons are supposed to meet as a staff planning group, for example, this kind of arrangement should be described and explained.

This section affords an opportunity to demonstrate administrative and managerial ability and know-how. It will give the reader confidence that the operation will be efficiently managed.

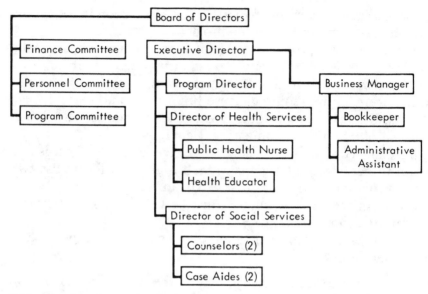

Figure 6. Sample organizational chart.

STAFFING

In some cases it may be expeditious and clearer to combine the material on staffing with the material from the previous section (on organizational structure) into a single major section with subsections. In other cases a separate section may work better. In any case each staff position should be listed with a brief description of responsibilities and qualifications. For each position the level of effort, such as full time, half time, 100 days must be indicated. It is not necessary to show salaries here: They will be in the budget. In addition, the manner in which the staff is organized should be described in terms of lines of responsibility, unless this has been done in the prior section of the proposal. An organization chart can also be used to further clarify these arrangements.

An example of how to set up the staff descriptive list follows:

One Project Director, full time, twelve months.

Responsibilities: Overall planning, direction, coordination, management and supervision of the program; liaison with community agencies and organizations; advocacy on behalf of clients; management of fiscal affairs; interpretation of policies and procedures to the community; staffing board committees; supervision of program coordinators.

Qualifications: Graduate degree in human services, such as social work; minimum of five years' experience in program supervision and management.

One Program Coordinator for Counseling, full time, twelve months.

Responsibilities: Direction of all counseling and therapy activities; supervision of counseling staff (psychologists and social workers); planning and implementation of in-service staff training programs; establishment of referral procedures with community agencies.

Qualifications: Graduate degree in human services, such as social work or psychology; minimum of three years' experience in provision and supervision of clinical services.

Two Social Workers, full time, twelve months.

Responsibilities: Direct work with families accepted for services; initial intake evaluation of families applying for service; provision of individual and group counseling for families; maintaining case records; assignment of children to clinical psychologist for individual care when necessary; referral to community agencies; participation in program evaluation activities; participation in staff supervisory conferences.

Qualifications: Master's degree from accredited school of social work with specialization in counseling or case work; minimum of two years' experience.

Two Clinical Psychologists, half time each, twelve months.

Responsibilities: Direct work with individual children accepted for treatment and with their families in individual and group sessions; establishing and implementing service plans for each client; administering psychological tests; referral to other agencies; maintaining case records; participation in program evaluation activities; participation in staff supervisory conferences.

Qualifications: Advanced degree and certification in clinical psychology.

An alternative to the preceding narrative format is to use listings of responsibilities and qualifications. The listing would look like this:

One Project Director, full time, twelve months.

Responsibilities:
Overall planning, direction, coordination, management, and supervision of program.
Liaison with community agencies and organizations.
Client advocacy.
Management of fiscal affairs.
Interpretation of policies and procedures to the community
Staffing board committees.
Supervision of program coordinators.
Qualifications:
Graduate degree in human services.
Minimum of five years' experience in program supervision and management.

Longer complete job specifications or descriptions for each position are sometimes asked for by funders. They should be given in an appendix and referred to in this section. Similarly, if it is known which persons will fill various jobs, their names should be included in this section and their full résumés attached in an appendix.

In this part of the proposal any special aspects of the approach to staffing the proposed program that have not been covered earlier can be discussed as well. For example, if the program stresses using an interdisciplinary approach to providing services, an explanation can be given here why this approach is being stressed and in which way the various staff responsibilities and qualifications serve to implement such an approach. If certain professional or experiential competencies among the staff are being stressed, an explanation of that approach can be given here and the manner in which the staffing pattern implements such an approach can be pointed out.

An example of how this can be done follows:

As we stressed in the section of the proposal on program activities, the provision of effective counseling for older people is highly dependent on the special abilities of the counseling staff. This staff must be able to communicate effectively with older people, to relate constructively to this group, and to have the technical skills to locate and marshal the necessary housing, health, recreational, educational, cultural, and income-maintenance services they require. For these reasons, we have built these abilities into the job descriptions presented below as aspects of both the job responsibilities and qualifications for each counseling position. Although we will employ staff without regard to any age qualifications, we are confident that the approach will result in a staff of primarily older persons who hold professional degrees in the counseling area.

This approach to staffing the project is consistent with and contributes to the achievement of the program objectives (described earlier in the proposal) aimed at providing role models for older people in the delivery of human services. The following is a description of each position.

This kind of explanation, which should appear early in the staffing section of the proposal, not only sets forth the organization's approach with respect to staffing but ties this approach up to both the program's objectives and the specific job descriptions. This contributes to the internal consistency of the proposal; it indicates careful program planning on the part of the proposing organization.

TIMETABLE

To include a section on timing strengthens the proposal and supports the program and organizational plan. The section should explain how long the program will last and when each activity will begin and end. This can best be done by using a GANTT or MILESTONE chart as shown in Figure 7.

Each activity described in the program or methods section of the proposal should be listed on the left side, with a line and arrow showing the start and the end of the activity. This is a GANTT chart. If a triangle ($\triangle$) is used instead of an arrow, it is usually referred to as a MILESTONE chart. In addition to the chart, a few paragraphs of narrative must be included summa-

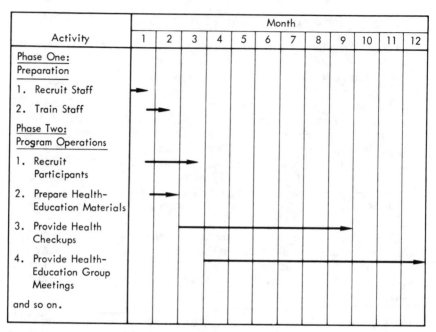

Figure 7. Sample timetable using a GANTT chart.

rizing the timetable. Aspects of the timetable that may not be clear from the chart, particularly the relationship between the timing for different activities, have to be explained. For example, if a month is needed to organize a board or committee before staff can be recruited, this should be noted to explain why the staff recruiting does not begin until the second month. If there is an evaluation activity, the rationale for starting it at the particular time indicated in the chart must be given. This type of explanation makes the timetable clearer to the funder and it demonstrates the applicant's understanding of the intricacies of program management.

A degree of confusion exists about the terminology used by some funders in requiring a timetable. These funders may refer to the necessity of including a PERT chart in the proposal. PERT stands for Program Evaluation Review Technique. It is a more complex, often computer-aided method for identifying the relationship and dependence over time among a wide variety of tasks. It was originally developed for use in construction pro-

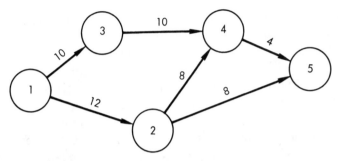

Figure 8. Example of PERT format.

jects. PERT is generally an inappropriate method for expressing timetables for relatively small service programs. When "PERT" is referred to, in reality often a very complete GANTT or MILE-STONE presentation is meant. A PERT chart in its most simple form is shown in Figure 8.

In a PERT chart the numbered circles represent a sequence of events, such as:

1. Approval of grant
2. Approval of job descriptions
3. Hiring of staff
4. Training of staff
5. Beginning of program

The numbers in the event circles do not represent time; they are used simply to identify events.

The arrowed lines represent the necessary activities that connect these events. The events represent the start or completion of the activity. The numbers on the lines represent the time period (number of days) to progress from one event to the next.

EVALUATION PLAN

If there is to be an evaluation as part of the proposed program, it should be described in a separate section that sets forth how it will be accomplished. Some proposal writers include this as a subsection of the program description section.

Funders vary as to their requirements for a formal evaluation of the program. If an evaluation is required or believed desirable, it often causes considerable consternation for proposal writers who are unfamiliar with the research and evaluation techniques required. It even troubles those who do know these techniques, because they recognize that (1) the characteristics of many social programs are not susceptible to a conclusive evaluation of effectiveness; (2) the requirements for reliable evaluation of social programs are quite complex; and (3) the resources usually made available for a proper evaluation are inadequate for the requirements.

It is necessary to be clear about the primary purpose of the evaluation. Is it mainly to assess the effectiveness of program methods or approaches that are being demonstrated? Is it to provide funders with a basis for considering refunding or funding additional similar work? Is it to meet a legislative requirement? Is it to ascertain the effectiveness of one program approach compared to another type of approach aimed at the same problem? Is it to be used as a feedback mechanism, so that changes in program methods can be instituted while the project is still going on? Is it primarily intended as a mechanism to provide increased accountability to the funder? The answers to these questions will help determine the nature and extent of evaluative activities to be built into the proposal.

It is important to identify the *level* of evaluation required by a funder or, if not required, that one still wants to include as a component of the proposal. The term "evaluation" often means different things. Clarity about what is meant and expected is the first step in preparing the evaluation section.

Evaluation can range from complex experimental research to relatively simple reporting and program-accounting activities. To evaluate the impact of a human service program by comparing a group that is served with a similar group that is not served is quite a different problem from providing reports on the number and characteristics of people served each month.

When program evaluation is a component of the proposal, the trend is to design the evaluation as either a process evaluation or an outcome evaluation, or both. The process evaluation focuses on how the program will be implemented by describing and assessing what services will be provided, how they will be provided, how many people will be served, the characteristics of those served, and what the strengths and weaknesses of the implementation are likely to be. The outcome, or impact evaluation as it is sometimes called, focuses on the results of the process including what the impact was on those served, what changes occurred in their behavior or life circumstances, what benefits were realized as a result of the program activities, and quantitative and qualitative measurement of the extent to which the program's objectives were attained. The most useful evaluations often combine the two approaches.

There are a number of different ways to approach the evaluation section of the proposal. One way is to demonstrate understanding of the complexity of evaluation and of its significance and its limitations. Then it must be indicated that an evaluation will be built largely around measuring the degree of effectiveness in accomplishing the program objectives and that a major preparatory activity during the first month or two after funding will be to prepare a complete evaluation design that will be submitted to the funding source.

In taking this approach it is essential to list the tasks that would be undertaken to produce such a complete design. These tasks include:

1. Defining each project objective in operational terms, susceptible to measurement

2. Developing the measurements that would be used as indicators of achievement of objectives and impact

3. Identifying variables that influence program performance and outcome

4. Specifying data requirements and identifying the source for each type of required data

5. Explaining the instruments that would be required and the method by which they would be developed and pretested

6. Describing the way in which the data would be obtained, that is, the data-collection methods

7. Discussing any sampling that would be done

8. Indicating the kinds of data analysis that would be undertaken

9. Describing the content of the final report

10. Describing the staffing and managing of the evaluation

11. Developing a timetable for the evaluation

It may be necessary to go beyond this list and to indicate the substance of a more complete design in the proposal. This means including a description of the kinds of measurements and data that would be used to describe the process and assess progress in accomplishing objectives. One would also need to outline the specific sources of such data and describe the kinds of methods and instruments (for instance, questionnaires, interview guides, and so on) that would be developed to collect the data. The way in which these instruments would be pretested must be explained.

It is advisable to try to retain a degree of flexibility in relation to the evaluation methods outlined in the proposal, unless one is very sure of the research techniques that will be used.

The use of both qualitative and quantitative measures should be stressed. For the first year of a program, it is wise to indicate that *progress* in achieving objectives will be assessed and measured rather than *ultimate* measures of effectiveness. This is appropriate, since most programs take more than one year to really prove themselves. This approach is called *formative* evaluation (as contrasted to *summative* evaluation) in that it contributes to the refinement or modification of program methods during the course of the program. At the same time, however, the funder must be assured that there will be concrete measures of the progress being made.

It is a helpful technique in the presentation to list each objective and to indicate the type of data that will be assembled and the method by which the data will be obtained.

For example:

Objective One: to increase interagency coordination
   EVALUATION MEASURES
      Quantitative data: Frequency of interagency meetings
      Qualitative data: Perceptions of agency executives regarding change in interagency working relationships and communication

DATA-COLLECTION METHODS

1. Review and tabulation of information from minutes of meetings (Explain how this will be done.)
2. Interviews with agency executives (Explain the way in which executives will be chosen, sampling if any), and the way in which interviews will be conducted.

When an evaluation section is included, the staffing section of the proposal must definitely show which staff members are responsible for design and implementation of the evaluation. If consultants are to be used, this should be explained. All the costs must be shown in the budget.

It will strengthen the presentation to indicate that periodic (monthly or quarterly) progress reports will be prepared. The accountability aspects of the operation are thereby reinforced. Federal, state, and local governmental agencies that fund programs, as well as some foundations, often have formal reporting requirements.

Another trend in evaluation is to provide information on the cost of various program activities and to relate these costs to the effectiveness of activities. This approach can be taken even further in the sense of attempting to estimate, in dollars, the benefits to clients or to the community that are derived from various programs. These dollar benefits can then be compared to costs. Cost-effectiveness and benefit–cost studies and analyses are complex research designs. The ability to generate reliable and valid cost and benefit data for human service programs is a perplexing problem even to the most sophisticated researchers. Nevertheless, an evaluation approach is strengthened if some data of this type are included. The simplest kind of data would be to estimate the total cost for each major set of program activities within the total program. One can also compute unit costs, that is, the cost for each person served. These kinds of data can then be related to information on the extent to which objectives are achieved.

Another approach to the evaluation problem is to use a "third party" or outside evaluator. This involves retaining one or more consultants, a consulting organization, or a university to design and carry out the evaluation. In such a case the evaluation design and estimated cost for evaluation may be prepared by the prospective outside evaluators and included as part of the total proposal.

The evaluation section should always explain how the collected information will be analyzed and reported. A general outline of the headings that can be expected in the final evaluation report may be included.

Given the latitude of possibilities of what might be included in the evaluation section, it is highly desirable to obtain some guidelines from the prospective funding source of its evaluation requirements and expectations. These are sometimes spelled out in RFPs, program announcements, or other written instructions from the funder. If they are not, a personal contact should be made to obtain more information.

In summary, a complete evaluation section is really a subproposal that contains most of the elements of a research proposal as described in chapter 6.

BUDGET AND BUDGET EXPLANATION

The budget is a representation of estimated expenses and income of the program expressed in dollar amounts. Many government funding agencies have their own forms that must be used in submitting the budget to them. Figures 9 and 10 show a sample budget and a federal budget form. The basic format discussed below (and shown in Figure 9) and the suggested methods for estimating costs will be useful in completing the forms used by government agencies as well as in preparing budgets for foundations. Most foundations do not prescribe a budget form to be filled out.

Funding agencies are concerned not only with the amount of money requested but also with the question whether the request is realistic and well justified. Correct presentation of the budget can help to convince funders of the proponent's managerial and administrative skills and capability. As with all other parts of the proposal, the more that can be learned about the rules and procedures followed by the funding agency, the more the proposal can be made responsive to the funding agency's requirements.

In addition to the budget itself, one should attach budget-explanation notes or sheets to explain the basis upon which budget items that are not self-explanatory have been estimated. These explanatory notes should be on a separate sheet(s) headed "Budget Explanation."

One of the most perplexing problems facing all proposal writers is the issue of "padding" the budget by requesting more than is needed. Padding is done on the assumption that funders cut almost all budget requests by some amount. Since funders can generally recognize padding, it is not recommended. A realistic budget that is optimistic in terms of the estimated expenditures is more desirable. Although it may be subject to some reduction, this type of request enhances the proposer's credibility with the funder.

On occasion, funders reduce a budget to a total amount that would really make it unrealistic or impossible for the applicant to carry out the program effectively. It is always tempting to accept even a drastically reduced grant rather than nothing, but experience has shown that this can be a mistake. It results only in problems later on in the project. Grant seekers must be willing to say "no" to unrealistic cuts. Funders will respect them for taking such a position. Done diplomatically, it can be a positive factor in their consideration of the next request.

One of the most important principles in preparing the budget is to be sure that it corresponds to the proposal's narrative material. The personnel budget must include all of the positions described in the staffing section. One should never show a salary for a position not previously discussed. The budget should be consistent with the activities listed in the program activities section. For example, one should not put an item in the budget for publication costs unless the narrative indicated that one of the activities will be to publish a report, newsletter, or other type of publication.

The major aspects of all budgets are expenses (or costs), income, and in-kind (or donated) items. These are explained below and illustrated in the sample budget in Figure 9.

EXPENSES

Personnel

Salaries

Executive Director 12 mos. @ $50,000 per annum	$50,000
Program Director 9 mos. @$32,000 per annum	24,000
Counselor 12 mos. @ $ 28,000 per annum	28,000
Secretary 6 mos. @ $20,000 per annum	10,000
Total Salaries	112,000

Fringe Benefits

Calculated @ 25% of salaries of $112,000 (See Budget Explanation Note)	28,000

Consultants

Medical Consultant 10 days @ $500 per diem	5,000
Marketing Consultant 10 days @ 400 per diem	4,000
Total Personnel	$149,000

Other Than Personnel

Office Rental 10,000 sq. ft. @ $3.00 ft.	30,000
Telephone 3 instruments @ $100 per mo. for 12 mos.	3,600
Travel 5,000 mi.@ .27 = $1,350 2 round trips N.Y-DC @ $200 = 400	1,750
Supplies (See Budget Explanation Note)	2,000
Equipment (See Budget Explanation Note)	4,000
Printing and Duplicating	1,000
Total Other Than Personnel	$42,350
Total Direct Expenses	$191,350

Indirect Expenses

Calculated @ 25% of salaries of $112,000 (See Budget Explanation Note)	$ 28,000
TOTAL EXPENSES	$219,350

INCOME

Fees (Basis Explained in Budget Explanation Note)	$10,000	
Total Income		$10,000

SUMMARY

Total Expenses	$219,350
Less Income	-10,000
NET REQUEST	$209,000

Figure 9.   Sample operating budget.

EXPENSE BUDGET

The expense budget includes the following:

PERSONNEL

The personnel category includes three separate items: (1) all wages and salaries paid to full- and part-time staff considered regular employees, (2) fringe benefits or employee benefits, (3) payment to consultants, other nonregular employees, or contractors.

SALARIES.   List each position, time devoted to program, annual salary rate, and budgeted amount. For example

SALARIES	AMOUNT
One executive director, twelve months, full time @ $50,000 per annum	$50,000
One nurse, twelve months, half time @ $30,000 per annum	15,000

The best way to estimate salaries is to find out the range paid for similar jobs within the organization and in other organizations. Salaries in the upper half of this range should be selected to indicate one's intention to attract high-quality people and to follow progressive personnel practices.

BUDGET INFORMATION — Non-Construction Programs

OMB Approval No. 0348-0044

SECTION A – BUDGET SUMMARY

Grant Program Function or Activity (a)	Catalog of Federal Domestic Assistance Number (b)	Estimated Unobligated Funds		New or Revised Budget		
		Federal (c)	Non-Federal (d)	Federal (e)	Non-Federal (f)	Total (g)
1.		$	$	$	$	$
2.						
3.						
4.						
5. TOTALS		$	$	$	$	$

SECTION B – BUDGET CATEGORIES

6. Object Class Categories	GRANT PROGRAM, FUNCTION OR ACTIVITY				Total (5)
	(1)	(2)	(3)	(4)	
a. Personnel	$	$	$	$	$
b. Fringe Benefits					
c. Travel					
d. Equipment					
e. Supplies					
f. Contractual					
g. Construction					
h. Other					
i. Total Direct Charges (sum of 6a - 6h)					
j. Indirect Charges					
k. TOTALS (sum of 6i and 6j)	$	$	$	$	$
7. Program Income	$	$	$	$	$

Figure 10. Sample federal government budget form.

72

If salaries include a mid-year increase, this must be indicated in the budget-explanation notes. If funds are being requested for a one-year (twelve-months) period for a new program, it is doubtful that all the staff will start on the first day of the project. Therefore, the budgeted amount must be reduced accordingly. For example, a full-time secretary may be required at $24,000 a year but will not be hired until the second month of operation. The annual rate must be shown after the position, but only eleven months (i.e., $22,000) of actual salary should be included in the expenditure-amount column.

FRINGE BENEFITS. Fringe benefits represent the expenses for social security, retirement plans, health insurance, unemployment compensation, disability insurance, and other similar costs paid by the program. Any costs paid by the employees themselves should not be included in this item. Fringe benefits are generally shown as a percentage of salaries, with a note explaining what is included. Most large organizations already have a computed fringe-benefit rate, ranging from 15 to 30 percent of salaries. (Some proposal writers prefer to show each fringe item rather than to use a cumulative percentage. For example, an item such as social security taxes would appear under personnel.) Fringe benefits are not paid for services of contractors or consultants, since they are hired as private contractors on a per diem or unit-cost basis.

A sample budget-explanation note, explaining the fringe benefit rate, might look like this (figures used are for purpose of illustration and do not represent current rates):

FRINGE BENEFITS ON SALARIES AND WAGES

Social Security	7.6%
State Unemployment	2.0%
State Disability	0.2%
Workers' Compensation	0.3%
Employee Retirement Plan	8.0%
Group Health and Hospitalization	5.0%
Group Life Insurance	1.0%
Dental Insurance	0.5%
TOTAL	24.6%

CONSULTANTS. Each type of consultant, the rate of pay, and the number of workdays being budgeted must be listed as shown in the sample budget on page 70. Each consultant should have been described in the staffing section of the proposal. It weakens the proposal to put in a budget amount for "consultation" without specifically describing it and justifying it in the narrative.

Some government agencies and foundations have specific policies regarding the use of consultants and the rate of reimbursement. These can be ascertained by asking the funding agency staff for its written regulations regarding use of consultants and contract services.

OTHER DIRECT EXPENSES

The second major category of costs includes all other direct expenses. These are costs other than personnel. They are often referred to as OTPS (other than personnel services) or NPS (nonpersonnel services). Costs included are:

1. *Travel* by staff, consultants and, if necessary, by the program's board members and participants. The detail and justification for travel costs should be shown in the budget itself or in a budget-explanation note. Out-of-town or long-distance travel must be shown separately from local travel; mileage, car rentals, and air travel must appear as separate items under "travel." Some funders have recommended travel and subsistence rates that establish maximum amounts to be paid for mileage, meals, and lodging. These rates can be obtained by request.

2. *Subsistence or per diem.* This item represents the reimbursement to persons for hotel and meals. The budget should show the number of days to be reimbursed and the amount to be paid per day.

3. *Office supplies* (consumables) consist of stationery, mimeograph paper, duplicating supplies, pens, and the like.

4. *Program supplies* such as training materials, instructional material, training manuals, and similar items to be purchased should be shown as a separate item and explained in the notes.

5. *Equipment* represents desks, typewriters, copy machines, duplicators, and so on. Each item and its purchase or rental cost should be listed and the total shown in the expenditure column. Funders have varying policies with respect to the extent to which they will fund purchase or rental of equipment and these policies should be ascertained. An example of a typical equipment explanation follows:

Equipment to be purchased totals $3,000 and includes:
2 desks @ $500 each = $1,000
4 chairs @ $100 each = $400
1 typewriter @ $500 = $500
1 computer @ $1,100 = $1,100

6. *Telephone* (communications) should show the monthly estimate, number of instruments, and total expenditures (see Figure 9).

7. *Rent* (facilities) should show the cost of office-space rental (indicating the number of square feet and cost per foot) and the total annual expenditure (see Figure 9). If remodeling or renovation costs are involved, these should be shown as well.

8. *Other expenditure items* should be listed individually. These include postage, printing of reports, agency memberships in other organizations, special insurance, purchase of publications, utilities (if not included in rent), and computer costs.

9. *Miscellaneous.* Some successful proposals include a miscellaneous item in the budget, but it is much better to show every specific item of expense. If this is done, a "miscellaneous" item should not be necessary. It should be avoided if possible. Leaving it out shows the funder that careful planning has gone into the budget estimate.

INDIRECT EXPENSE

Indirect expense or overhead refers to the costs incurred by the larger agency within which the project occurs. If the proposed program or project is not part of a larger operation, it should not include any overhead items.

PERSONNEL SALARIES	FUNDS REQUESTED	IN-KIND (organization share)	TOTAL
Project Director—Full time @ $50,000 per an-num	$40,000	$10,000	$50,000
Asst. Director—Full time @ $36,000	$36,000		36,000
Research Asst.—One—quarter time @ $32,000		$8,000	$8,000

Figure 11. Sample format to show cost sharing by using in-kind contributions.

If a proposal is (1) for a program to be carried out as part of a larger operation, and (2) if the larger organization will provide certain administrative services such as payroll, office space, equipment, and so on, it is appropriate to include such costs as part of the budget. These expenses are figured as a percentage of salaries. Large organizations usually have a standard rate used for this purpose that may range from 10 to 100 percent. If the organization already has government contracts, this rate has most likely already been negotiated with government auditors. If one will not have such costs, this item should not be included in the budget.

IN-KIND CONTRIBUTIONS OR COST SHARING

Some funders expect the applying organization to share a part of the cost of a project. This may be done in two ways: through actual cash amounts or through in-kind contributions. Even if the funder does not require some matching contribution, it is often good strategy to show either income that will be raised or in-kind contributions of staff time or equipment. A sample format for showing these contributions is shown in Figure 11.

INCOME

Some proposed programs may have sources of income as part of their operation from fees, expected contributions, and so on. If this is true, then the estimated income must be shown as part of the total budget and subtracted from the expenses to reach a requested amount as shown in the sample budget in Figure 9.

FUNCTIONAL, PROGRAM, OR COST CENTER BUDGETS

Sometimes a funder may request a functional, program, or cost center budget in addition to the line-by-line budget illustrated in Figure 9. There are also times when it is advisable to prepare such a budget in order to clarify the relative costs of different aspects of a multifunction operation. This type of budget requires that the total expenditures be allocated to the major functions or program components.

The steps necessary to do this are:

First, prepare the line item budget.

Second, devise the major functional activities or program categories such as administration, intake, health education, community relations, counseling services, training, evaluation, and information and referral. In very complex programs a major program category can be further divided into subcategories. For example, counseling could be broken down into counseling youth, counseling adults, and counseling aging persons.

Third, estimate the proportion of each line item that can be appropriately allocated to each functional category. For example, an Associate Director at $40,000 a year might devote one-half time to administration, one-quarter time to community relations, and one-quarter time to health education. In such a case, one would allocate $20,000 to administration, $10,000 to community relations, and $10,000 to health education.

Fourth, add up the amounts that are allocated to each category.

Fifth, prepare a budget that shows all the categories and the total dollar cost for each category. Attach a budget-explanation sheet describing the detailed description of how the total for each category was reached.

CAPABILITY STATEMENTS

As indicated in earlier sections, it is essential to convey to the funder that the organization has the capability to carry out the proposed program effectively and efficiently. In part, this capability is established by the quality of the proposal itself. It is also dealt with directly by providing descriptive capability material in the proposal about the abilities, competence, resources, personnel, experience, record of successful achievements, viability, reputation, and philosophy of the organization. Some of this material may have been presented briefly in the introductory section of the proposal. References to capability may also have been made in the proposed program description and in describing the project staff. However, and especially in the case of large-scale requests, a separate part of the proposal that contains an overall capability statement is advisable. This statement can take the form of a section of the proposal or of an attachment or appendix. If it is decided to include a capability section, the reader's attention should be called to it in the letter of transmittal or in the introduction to the proposal.

Typically, a capability section should cover the following:

- Brief history of the organization; its reasons for starting; the time and place of its start; the source of funds; and the problem or need it seeks to address

- Overall philosophy, mission and/or goals of the organization

- Experience of the organization, including significant programs and achievements and its track record in obtaining prior grants

- Evidence of credibility, adherence to standards and ongoing support, such as total size and budget; membership in national organizations; meeting of incorporation, accreditation and/or standard-setting requirements; endorsements from officials and other organizations, agencies, and community groups, newspaper editorials or commendations; citations and reference to the organization's work in publications

- Organizational resources, including qualifications and background of staff; boards and committees; offices and equipment; ongoing administrative structure; mechanisms for financial and programmatic accountability

5

MINI-PROPOSALS AND PROPOSAL LETTERS

A NUMBER OF FOUNDATIONS AND A FEW GOVERNMENT FUNDERS SPEC-
ify that applicants should submit a short proposal in the form
of a letter or brief statement prior to submitting a full proposal
as described in chapter 4. In addition, some foundations that
make only small grants of under $5,000 or $10,000 may only
require submission of a letter proposal. Because of the increase
in the number of funding applications, increasing numbers of
funders have turned to using letter proposals as a way to review
proposals more efficiently.

Before sending a proposal to a funding source it is important
to obtain a copy of its grant application procedures. Review of
the way this material describes what the funder wants in a letter proposal will be very helpful in crafting the proposal. Funders refer to mini-proposals in a variety of ways including,
"letter of intent," "letter of inquiry," "preproposal letter," "proposal letter," "letter of interest," "preliminary outline," "project brief," "prospectus," and the like.

Some of the ways in which different foundations state their
procedures and requirements regarding the initial submission
of letter proposals include:

Before submitting a formal proposal, organizations may wish to contact a member of the staff or submit a brief summary of their project for initial review and discussion.

The foundation does not have grant application forms. To be considered for foundation aid, an institution or organization should write a one-or-two-page pre-proposal letter that describes the basic problem and the plan for its solution. The letter should briefly explain project objectives, operational procedures, time schedule, and personnel and financial resources available and needed.

We have found that the most effective way for us to give an informed response to an organization interested in applying for a grant is to review a brief letter of inquiry from the grant seeker . . . please be specific about the nature of your project; a basic proposal outline is helpful to us.

The foundation requires that organizations considering submission of a proposal to the foundation write a brief letter describing the applicant organization and summarizing the proposed project and the amount of support to be requested.

Letters of inquiry should contain no more than three pages with the following information: a description of the organization and a statement relating its purpose to the general interests and specific priorities of the foundation; a summary of the purpose for which the grant is being sought and evidence of the need for the activity; an overall operating budget and a detailed budget for the project.

Mini-proposals serve a number of functions. First, they provide a device to facilitate the initial screening of requests by funders, enabling the funder to judge the extent to which the proposed project is eligible for funds and whether it is consistent with the funder's interests, goals, and priorities. Mini-proposals may provide an opportunity for the funder to suggest modifications prior to submission of a complete proposal. They also provide a way to inquire about the possible interest of a number of different funders at the same time with a minimum of paperwork and preparation.

Some proposal writers recommend that the mini-proposal or letter should be submitted to funders whenever possible. However, unless the funding agency requires this as part of its funding process, there are some disadvantages to routinely employing the mini-proposal approach. Funders may be more inclined to disregard the receipt of a mini-proposal than of a complete proposal. Because of its brevity, it also has the disadvantage of possibly obscuring the impact or importance of a proposed project. Thus, one must weigh the pros and cons of this approach carefully. If in doubt, submit a more complete proposal with a good summary section as suggested in chapter 4.

In cases where a mini-proposal is clearly desirable or required, the following guidelines will aid its preparation.

FORMAT

The typical mini-proposal is two or three pages long. Some ways to increase the impact of a mini-proposal are:

- Use a few headings such as "Objectives," "Program," "Organization," and "Staff and Budget," if the mini-proposal is more than two pages long.

- Always include a formal title for the project.

- If the mini-proposal is more than three pages long, consider submitting it as a separate document with a brief cover letter.

- Keep attachments to a minimum by including only what the funder specifies. If you have an attractive annual report, consider sending that along.

- Include some breakdown of the budget rather than a single lump sum request.

- Address the letter to a specific individual by name. You can call the funder to find out the name and title of the person to whom you should address your request.

- Use white paper to assure legibility when duplicated.

- Do not justify the right-hand margin unless you have printing capability to assure proportional spacing.

ITEMS TO STRESS

Most mini-proposals should have a minimum of eight brief, substantive paragraphs, including:

1. A paragraph telling why the proposal should be of interest to the funder, that is, its responsiveness or consistency with the funder's stated goals, interests, or prior funding history.

2. A paragraph describing what the proposal is about, where the proposed activity will take place, who will be served, and the time period for the project.

3. A paragraph describing the background and capability of the organization.

4. A paragraph stating the major problem and need for the proposed project including a few key facts or data that document the need for or the extent of the problem.

5. A paragraph defining the overall purpose of the project and listing its major objectives.

6. A paragraph summarizing the major activities that will be undertaken.

7. A paragraph outlining the staff or personnel that would be paid from the grant, the use of volunteers, and in-kind staff contributions of the organization, if any.

8. A paragraph explaining the budget request.

It is often desirable to attach a one-page line-by-line budget, unless the request is quite small and is self-explanatory and based on the material in the mini-proposal itself, for example, a request for $2,000 for a needed computer or $3,000 to print the proceedings of an institute.

6

RESEARCH
PROPOSALS

THIS CHAPTER DESCRIBES THE CHARACTERISTICS OF RESEARCH PROPOS-
als and outlines methods for their preparation. It assumes that
the proposal writer has an introductory working knowledge of
the basic concepts and methods of social research including the
fundamentals of design, measurement, and the collection and
analysis of quantitative and qualitative data.

WHAT IS A RESEARCH PROPOSAL?

A research proposal is a specialized type of proposal to gain
financial support in order to obtain and analyze information to
describe and explain a particular problem, issue, subject, or
question. Research proposals may be for basic research aimed
at advancing knowledge. Or they may be for applied research to
examine behavior, attitudes, policies, programs, materials, procedures, or processes. Such research may contribute to a better
understanding of specific phenomena or may be used to provide

guidance for making decisions about policies, programs, procedures, operations, and finances. The principles and techniques included in this chapter focus primarily on applied research in fields such as health, mental health, social welfare, sociology, psychology, economics, the arts and humanities, education, community planning and the like. In these fields proposals may take a variety of forms, including:

Evaluations of programs and policies
Descriptive, analytic, and comparative studies of programs, organizations, materials, or methods
Surveys of population characteristics and public opinion
Case studies
Needs assessments
Market research
Investigations of a particular problem of phenomenon
Experiments and quasi-experiments
Demonstration and testing of research methods
Studies of costs, benefits, and effectiveness
Operations research
Historical analysis
Theory testing
Epidemiological studies
Cross-sectional studies
Longitudinal studies

In part, many of these distinctions are semantic. A study of the extent to which a training/work program has resulted in reduced welfare costs may be an evaluation, an analytic study, a case study, a cost-benefit analysis, and a cross-sectional study simultaneously. In preparing research proposals one of the first steps is to identify the primary purpose of the research and use this as a basis for identifying what kind of research is being proposed. Since there are usually a number of choices, one should consider selecting the kinds of research in which the potential funding sources have already demonstrated some interest in supporting.

MAKING RESEARCH PROPOSALS MORE EFFECTIVE

Research proposals are often subject to more intensive technical review than program proposals, especially proposals submitted to funders that have the support of research as their major focus, such as the National Institutes of Health and the National Science Foundation, two of the major federal agencies that support considerable research. The various research and development sections of the units and bureaus of all the major federal departments, such as HHS, HUD, Commerce, Agriculture, and Interior, have also been increasing the intensity of their review of the research and development proposals that they support. The same has been true among the larger foundations.

Many federal agencies and many state agencies and foundations that support research through grants and contracts use technical panels of reviewers from their own staff and of outside experts to rate proposals that have been submitted. Therefore the success of research proposals depends greatly on the extent to which they adhere to certain expectations or protocols that have become traditionally accepted in the field of research. At the same time, reviewers pay considerable attention to the extent to which new, innovative, and promising research approaches are incorporated into the proposal. One of the challenges the proposal writer faces is to write the proposal so that it adequately demonstrates a familiarity with the traditional methodological expectations yet promises to break new ground.

Because of their specialized nature, research proposals must meet certain requirements that differ from program proposals. There are seven major requirements for research proposals to which funders can be expected to pay particular attention. These include the need to effectively:

1. Describe the particular *problem* toward which the research is directed.

2. Review and discuss the relevant *related research and literature* pertinent to the problem being studied.

3. Explain the *significance* of the proposed research in terms of how it will further knowledge and contribute to the so-

lution of a substantive, theoretical, methodological, policy, organizational, or programmatic problem.

4. Define the *conceptual framework* for the proposed research, including the basic concepts involved, their relationships, and their operational or concrete manifestations.

5. Indicate the *specific research objectives* or questions that will be addressed or the specific hypotheses that will be tested.

6. Specify in detail the *research approach, methods, and procedures* that will be used to select subjects (i.e., persons, organizations or other units of analysis) and to obtain and analyze data.

7. Show the *capability* to conduct and complete the proposed work.

In addition, the research proposal should meet all of the criteria set forth in chapter 3.

The special characteristics of research proposals require that they follow a somewhat different format from other proposals. Research proposals should include the following components:

Letter of Transmittal
Title Page
Table of Contents
Abstract or Summary
Introduction, Topic, and Purpose
Statement of the Problem
Significance of the Research
Review of the Literature and Related Research
Theoretical Base and Conceptual Framework
Hypothesis, Objectives, and/or Questions
Research Design, Methods, and Procedures
Work Plan and Timetable
Organizational and Administrative Structure
Personnel (Staffing)
Budget and Budget Explanation
Capability Statement
Supporting Documents

The order and the organization of this material may vary considerably according to the particular kind of research problem and the research, design, and complexity. Some examples of different outlines for research proposals are presented later in this chapter.

Experience has shown that three sections of the research proposal are especially critical, and weaknesses in these sections often contribute to the failure of many proposals. These are the sections on (1) design and research procedures, (2) problem description, and (3) personnel. A lack of clarity, completeness, and consistency, and the presence of technical flaws are the main difficulties that arise in these sections. One can overcome such problems in several ways. First and foremost, be very sure that the proposal demonstrates a high level of technical research understanding and skill. Proposal writers should not hesitate to use consultants and seek advice of others in preparing the research design. One should examine other successful proposals and use reference books on research design as handy ways to check one's own work.

It is essential that the methods section explain both what will be done and fully describe how it will be done. One of the most difficult aspects of describing research methodology is to achieve a balance between the tendency to be too brief (listing the major procedures without explaining how they will be implemented) or being too detailed (presenting an array of ideas and the minutiae of technical procedures). To overcome this, it is helpful to break the methods section down into subsections, as outlined later in this chapter. Identify a central methodological approach. Don't try to cover every detailed procedure, but describe all major activities in a way that demonstrates their relevance to the study's objectives and establishes your technical competence. Discuss the limitations of the methodology and how expected methodological problems (e.g., interviewer bias or low return rate from a mail questionnaire) will be minimized.

A convincing and clear exposition of the problem, its significance, and a review of related work are indispensable for the success of the research proposal. It is impossible to write an adequate problem section without having done considerable investigation of the subject beforehand. Selective completeness is the key to success in this section—that is, citations and the discussion of the literature (theories and other research) should be limited to those directly relevant to the research. A tour de force of the literature is not what funders are looking for. A fewer number of relevant citations and an astute discussion of their relevance to the proposed research can be more effective than a long bibliography. At the same time, be certain that all major relevant work is mentioned in order to demonstrate that you are thoroughly conversant with the area. Talking and consulting with other persons in the field and asking them to review the material can help to ensure this section is as strong as possible. They can inform you of other research, suggest related theoretical work, and call attention to inaccuracies or lack of clarity. Make use of that most valuable but often underutilized resource person, the reference librarian. Use the various computer searches available at libraries to locate related material. However, be cautious in citing material from these searches without firsthand examination of the work. The computer search programs tend to turn up a good deal of material that may use key words similar to yours but may not really be related to your research project.

The main weaknesses in the staffing section that adversely affect a research proposal's chances of success are the lack of experience, training, or track record of the personnel conducting the research. The three principal ways to overcome this defect are to (1) be sure to fully describe the research capabilities of the personnel listed; (2) demonstrate one's research competence by making all other sections of the proposal as technically expert as possible; and (3) include research consultants who have impressive credentials as part-time members of the research staff, if necessary.

The remainder of this chapter outlines the various sections of the research proposal. A checklist of the specific material that should be covered in each section is provided along with suggested techniques for improving the effectiveness of each section. It is suggested that the reader supplement this material with the guidelines set forth in chapter 4.

LETTER OF TRANSMITTAL

A letter of transmittal should accompany a research proposal, even if the proposal is submitted on forms prescribed by the funding agency. A one- or two-page letter usually suffices unless you are using the letter as a mini-proposal or letter of inquiry (see chapter 5). The letter should contain:

- The names of the organization and researchers (with their organizational title and affiliation) submitting the proposal
- The RFP, program announcement, or funder interest to which the proposal responds
- A brief statement of the overall research strategy that will be utilized
- The amount being requested
- An indication of the special experience or capability of the proposer to successfully carry out the research
- How long the project will take to complete
- Willingness to discuss the proposal with the funder and consider modifications

The letter should put emphasis on succinct statements (two to four sentences each) of the problem, the significance of the research, and the overall research strategy, design, or approach. If the proposed research is based on prior research one has done, this should also be emphasized in the letter of transmittal.

TITLE PAGE

The title page for a research proposal follows the same format as that for program proposals shown on page 30. Special care should be taken in devising the title for a research proposal since it represents, in effect, a very brief summary of the proposal. Another reason titles are important is that the title words may be used to list the research in the various computerized abstract and search systems used to identify research information. Therefore, the title should include words descriptive and relevant to the specific subject being studied.

The title page should include:

The title of the research
Names and addresses of the submitting agency and names of principal investigators
Date submitted
Budget request total

Certain common errors in titling research proposals should be avoided. One is the tendency to make titles too global and imply that the research will provide the definitive answer to a major problem, when in effect it is directed toward only one aspect of the problem. For example, a title such as "A Study to Determine the Causes of Unemployment" promises something that has eluded most social and economic research. A more appropriate and descriptive title might be "A Study of Social Factors Associated with Unemployment of Urban Youth."

A second mistake in titling research proposals is the tendency toward unnecessary technical mystification. Remember that the majority of research projects in the social, behavioral, cultural, economic, and political fields will be reviewed by staff, reviewers, and panels that may include some persons who are not experts in the specific area of the proposal. In addition, funded proposals are often listed in foundation reports, or federal agencies may report them to members of Congress. It is no great honor to be selected for an award for an obtuse or overly grandiose title. Avoid jargon and ambiguity in the title. Avoid provoking unnecessary political sensitivity.

Follow the title page with a table of contents listing each heading and page number as described earlier on page 34.

ABSTRACT

The summary of a research proposal is called an Abstract. This summary statement may be 150 to 500 words. Many federal agencies require 200 or 250 words. The ideal summary is about one typewritten page, double spaced. Although the abstract appears at the beginning of the proposal it is usually the last part to be written.

It should include brief statements and paraphrases of only the most salient aspects of the proposal related to:

- The problem and its significance
- The purpose and objectives or hypotheses
- Reference to the major prior research
- The overall research approach (such as case study, experiment, comparative study, and so on)
- Its scope (what or who will be studied)
- The major procedural emphasis (interviews, field observations, questionnaires) and the analytical approach that will be used
- Expected outcomes

When writing the abstract, include some of the key words used in the proposal narrative to sensitize the reader to the most important themes. Do the abstract carefully since it is usually the first part that is read; sometimes it is the only part read by some reviewers. In addition, the abstract (along with the title) may be used in the various national computerized information systems, so major reference terms should appear in the abstract.

Abstracts are difficult for proposal writers to prepare. They are so close to and involved with all of the material in the proposal that it is hard to select only the key material. One way to overcome this problem is to time the writing of the proposal so that it can be put aside for a day or two before writing the abstract. Most writers start with abstracts that are too long. Combining sentences, omitting unnecessary qualifying words, and simply deleting entire sentences are ways to cut down on the length.

INTRODUCTION AND PURPOSE

The first part of the narrative is the introductory material. Some proposal writers omit this section since it may duplicate the abstract or letter of transmittal. In this case they start with the statement of the problem. If you decide you want a general introduction, begin with a few sentences that indicate what the proposal is about, its overall purpose, and the RFP number or specific program or interest of the funder to which the proposal is a response. Briefly summarize the essence of the problem and the research objectives and approach that will be used. In the case of research proposals the statement of purpose can be short and descriptive, such as "to conduct an evaluation of outpatient clinics" or "to examine the determinants of cost overruns among training programs." Such descriptive statements of purpose can be improved by adding an overall outcome, such as "... to determine the impact of their services ..." or "... to devise cost-control mechanisms. ... " Mention any prior research you have conducted that represents a precursor to the proposed study. Finally, explain how the remainder of the proposal is organized.

Some proposal writers prefer to use most of the introduction to explain the capability of the researchers and their institution in some detail. The introduction is also a good place to point out how the proposal is directly related to other work funded by the grant program to which one is applying. Funders are attracted to efforts that represent continuity or an extension of successful projects they have funded in the past. If the prior work was unsuccessful or wasteful, it is important to differentiate the proposed research from that done earlier by other investigators.

THE PROBLEM AND ITS SIGNIFICANCE

The research proposal should focus on a specific aspect of one main topic of study, such as characteristics of homeless persons, hospital workers' attitudes toward AIDS, comparison of costs for short-term and long-term counseling, drug use among high-school youth, and the like. Start this section of the proposal by describing and elaborating the main topic. The topic should be discussed as a research problem in the sense that there are unanswered or elusive questions about the topic and a need for more description, information, experimentation, or analysis. Then go on to describe the particular factors associated with the topic that will be the subject of the research. The problem section of the research proposal is similar to the needs section of other types of proposals as described in chapter 4.

The problem statement should cover three main interrelated points which may be all discussed in one section of the proposal, as separate subsections, or as individual sections with their own headings. The organization of this material will depend on the nature of the problem and one's writing style. The most important thing is to be sure that all three points are covered, presented in clear language, well documented, and responsive to the requirements of the RFP or the interests of the funder. The points are:

- The nature or characteristics of the problem, including what is known about it, and the conception of the problem that is being used in the proposal
- The extent of the problem and why the problem is or should be of interest and importance
- The usefulness of gaining additional knowledge related to the problem

The following are some guidelines to help present each of these points more effectively.

THE NATURE OR CHARACTERISTICS OF THE PROBLEM

An explanation of the nature of the problem is a way of defining the topic to make it susceptible to research. It is the beginning of developing the study's conceptual framework. The key to doing this is to identify and explain the relationship, influence, or effects of certain other factors (or variables) on the problem. For example, in explaining a topic such as student achievement in school, one might define it in terms of the effects of class size, student-teacher ratios, socioeconomic class, school facilities, and so forth. Or one might examine it in terms of textbook selection, library facilities, teacher qualifications, and such. In this way the topic is translated into a problem about which there is a need to determine the relationship or influence of these factors (variables) on certain outcomes, situations, or behaviors. Use the literature to document the factors and relationships you choose to include in the research.

THE EXTENT OF THE PROBLEM

The problem can be further elaborated by providing quantitative and/or qualitative information on its scope and extent. The number, distribution, rate, and trends in school dropouts, street crime, divorce, stress-related illnesses, or youth unemployment are examples of the kinds of data that can be used to elaborate the problem definition. Using these kinds of data also highlights the importance of the problem and, by extension, the importance of the proposed research.

In addition to describing the extent of the problem, it helps to document the professional and/or public interest in the problem by referring to other research, journal articles, commission reports, legislative mandates, newspaper articles, and similar material. Pointing out the effects and costs of the problem to individuals, the economy, the government, the society, and institutions is an additional way to emphasize its importance.

USEFULNESS AND APPLIED VALUE

Because proposal writers and researchers are so very convinced of the importance of what they are doing, they often have a tendency to assume that the value of the research being proposed is self-evident. This is an error. It is necessary to be explicit about the significance of the proposed research by explaining in what ways it will contribute to a further understanding of the problem. One should specify how the outcomes of the research can be applied value in the design of methods, material, policies, programs, or operations. Including this kind of information also prepares the reader for the later discussion of the specific research objectives or hypotheses.

REVIEW OF THE LITERATURE

Additional knowledge about the understanding of social problems takes place primarily as the result of either an extension of prior work or a criticism of prior ideas and approaches. It is important, therefore, to pay considerable attention to the section of the proposal that reviews the theories and the prior research and work related to the problem under study. This discussion can be enhanced by approaching the review of the literature not as a perfunctory obligation to the norms or research, but as a way of emphasizing the importance of the proposed research, adding richness to the problem discussion, identifying the state of the art, and helping justify the later description of the research design.

The following guidelines can enhance the effectiveness of this section. These include:

- Be thorough but relevant—cover all of the major work, but do not attach long bibliographies of every possible citation
- Group the related literature—use categories built around different types of theories and different methodological approaches; or group it in terms of the key variables or concepts that will appear in the design
- Be critical and fair—discuss related work in terms of its strengths and weaknesses and point out the basis for these conclusions
- Illustrate how the proposed study builds on the prior work by replicating, extending, modifying, or challenging it through an alternative approach

Depending on the flow of the narrative, one may also develop the study's conceptual framework here by describing each of the key concepts that is part of the study if those concepts are based on the literature being reviewed.

OBJECTIVES OR HYPOTHESES

A separate section of the proposal should state the specific objectives of the study, the hypotheses to be tested, or the questions to be answered or addressed. Any or all of these may be addressed, and the section may be located either before or after the explanation of the problem and the literature review. It should precede the design, procedures, or methods section of the proposal.

Hypotheses are always stated in terms of expected or predicted relationships among variables that will be tested—for example: "Stress levels will be significantly greater for executives than for assembly-line workers." Hypotheses must be linked to and supported by the theoretical and empirical knowledge base discussed in the section that reviews the related literature and defines key concepts. Formal hypotheses are most appropriate in studies where they can be subjected to statistical tests of significance. Hypotheses are, in effect, statements of the expected knowledge that will be an outcome of the study. It is seldom necessary to include null hypotheses in the proposal (even though they may be used in the analysis).

Objectives, on the other hand, are less formal outcome statements that do not speculate about the specific character of the expected relationships or findings. Instead, objectives are statements about what the research will achieve. An example would be: "The study will ascertain the extent to which the training program is reaching low-income persons" or "The study will identify the distribution of stress among executives and assembly-line workers."

In some cases neither the specification of hypotheses or objectives may be appropriate. In such cases one should at least state the questions that will be answered. For example,

> The study will address the following questions: Are schools adhering to federal guidelines? Who are the principal school officials involved in policy decisions?

It should be apparent from the foregoing examples that as one moves from hypothesis to objectives to questions, the definition of a study's final outcomes becomes less precise. Thus, one should rely on the question format only in the case of studies of an exploratory nature and where it is not possible or desirable to be too specific about key variables. Otherwise, always use objectives unless hypotheses are called for by the design. Proposal writers frequently fail to recognize the ease with which questions can be converted to objectives. For example, a question such as "Were the classroom materials used suitably?" can be restated as an objective: "To determine the extent to which suitable materials were used in the classroom." Except in the case of exploratory studies, one should always use a statement of specific objectives in the proposal. If it is an experimental or quasi-experimental design using quantitative measures, the proposal should include formal hypotheses. Any good research text describes the characteristics and rules for the statement of hypotheses.

When stating the objectives of a research project, present them in list form. They should meet the criteria outlined in chapter 3. In addition to objectives stating what the study will substantively achieve (e.g., "determine the cost of the program"), there should also be one or more objectives regarding the report of the study and its dissemination. This is usually at the end of a list of objectives. An example would be:

> To prepare a final report of procedures, findings, and conclusions and recommendation for submission to the Foundation and to agencies in the field.

If conferences or workshops are to be held or other devices for dissemination to be used, these should also be indicated as one of the objectives.

When stating objectives, always use active words and state them as outcomes of the research; for example, "to determine the extent of duplication among programs" is better than "to examine duplication among programs." Only include objectives related to points made in the discussion of the problem. Only include objectives feasible within the resources, time, and data base that will be obtained as outlined in the section of the proposal on design and procedures. Gear the presentation of objectives to the potential applied contribution of the study to the interests of the funding source. For example, if a funding program has a stated interest in "urban problems," include reference to "urban problems" in the discussion of the objectives.

RESEARCH DESIGN AND PROCEDURES

In practice, the term "research design" is used in a variety of ways. It is sometimes used to refer to the entire proposal, sometimes to research procedures, sometimes to the type of design (e.g., experimental design). Similarly, research procedures and research methods are used in different ways and sometimes are used interchangeably.

There are many different ways to organize and present the material to describe the research approach and methods to be employed. A good deal depends on the nature and complexity of the problem and of the design. Regardless of how one organizes this material, six specific elements should be presented, including:

- A description of the type of overall design to be used and why it has been adopted
- Definitions of concepts and how they will be put into effect
- Delineation of the variables or data categories, how they will be controlled, and what their relationships are
- A description of the data sources, including populations or other units to be studied and how the sources will be selected
- A description of the data to be collected and the methods and procedures to be applied
- A plan for analyzing the data and their presentation

Each of these elements is discussed in the remainder of this chapter.

OVERALL DESIGN

There is a wide variety of choices of overall design for social research. The proposal is improved by clearly stating the type of study approach being proposed, its general characteristics, why it is appropriate, its feasibility, and its limitations.

Research designs may be categorized in a number of ways. One way is based on the extent to which causal or associated relationships are or are not identified. Studies in which relatively little is known ahead of time about the variables involved are exploratory or formulative studies. As one can be more specific in the design with respect to variables, the study may be called a descriptive, analytic, or evaluative study. As the degree of control over variables increases, the design may be referred to as experimental or quasi-experimental.

Study design may also be characterized by other methodological approaches. That is, whether they are case studies, experiments, comparative, longitudinal, cross-sectional, participant observer, sample surveys, among others. The overall research approach should be given a label, such as "a descriptive-analytic study of ..." or "an evaluation of ..." It should be described and discussed in terms of why it has been selected, its appropriateness, and feasibility in connection with achieving the objectives of the study.

All researchers would like to obtain results that are as conclusive as possible. Some proposal reviewers may begin with this mindset and the assumption that the "pure" experimental design is the sought-for ideal, since it supposedly offers the most control over variables. This seems to be true, even though there is abundant literature of the weaknesses, to say nothing of the lack of feasibility, of the experimental approach in applied studies of social, economic, and political phenomena. To overcome this possibility, it is important to be specific about the way in which the selected research approach will produce the kind of data and analyses required to realize the objectives of the study. In explaining why the approach is appropriate, also refer to the literature and other studies and to the state of the art, helping to further legitimate the choice of design.

EXPLICATION OF VARIABLES

The design section is strengthened by a detailed discussion of the variables to be studied. A variable is a general class or category of objects, processes, structures, events, information, behaviors, or characteristics. As such, it is an abstraction. Each of the variables to be studied should be specified, and the empirical or observable characteristics (i.e., the operational definitions) that will be used to represent the variable should be delineated. There is always a good deal of latitude in operationalizing variables. For example, a variable such as "health professionals" might be defined as persons holding a degree in medicine, nursing, dentistry, or allied health. It could be further defined as persons working in health agencies (hospitals, clinics) who hold such a degree. In developing an operational definition, be sure that it is directly relevant to the way the problem has been defined and the way the objectives (or hypotheses) have been stated. Research proposals often are faulted for a lack of internal consistency, and it behooves any proposal writer to take great care that the material in this section of the proposal is consistent with the other sections.

In discussing variables it is productive to group them into appropriate categories, such as "dependent, independent, and intervening variables," or "input and output variables," or "benefit and cost variables" or "family, individual, and community variables," or whatever other general categories may best suit the overall design. Use these categories as subheadings in the narrative description of the variables.

The expected relationships among variables should also be described and the way the study will ascertain the extent of these relationships should be briefly mentioned here, even though this will be discussed in more detail later in the data analysis section of the proposal.

The discussion of variables and their relationships is, in effect, the presentation of a conceptual and operational model of the problem or phenomena being researched. One can supplement the narrative with a graphic illustration of this material as a summary and in order to add clarity and impact. A sample research graphic is shown in Figure 12.

SCOPE, UNITS OF ANALYSIS, AND DATA SOURCES

The explanation of the study design should include a description of exactly what units (or subjects) will be studied, how they will be selected, how many will be studied, and where they are located. This material, along with the later discussion of what data will be collected, clarifies the scope of the study.

Indicate whether the primary units to be studied are individuals, groups, organizations, activities, policies, materials, books, and so on. The characteristics of these units should be described further by factors such as their demography (age, sex, etc.), geography (location), time, or other factors. It is surprising how frequently proposal writers fail to specify this fundamental aspect of a study, thinking it is self-evident.

How the units to be studied will be selected should be described in detail. In a study of individual opinion or behavior, it is often necessary to sample populations. In these cases, outline the sampling methodology and indicate whether it will be

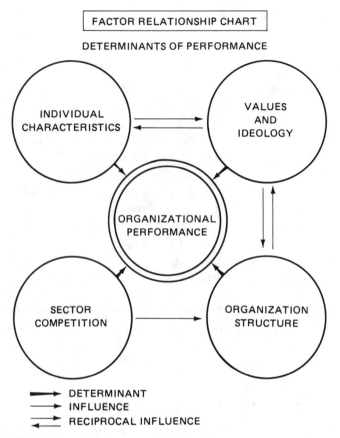

Figure 12. Sample research chart.

a probability sample involving randomization or a nonprobability sample (such as snowball, judgmental, quota, exemplary cases). Include each step in the selection process and any statistical devices that will be used in selecting random samples. If samples are other than random, the steps in the selection process should still be explained. If organizations or programs are to be studied, specify what units, departments, offices, or activities will be examined and how and why these will be selected.

DATA BASE, MEASUREMENT, AND INSTRUMENTATION

The design should specify how each variable will be measured through the use of tests, instruments, interviews, field observations, or other methods. If ratings, indices, and scoring devices are used, these should be explained. This section should describe how the variables (i.e., what is to be measured) will be represented by specific sets of data. If tests, interview guides, and questionnaires are to be used, the data items included in the instrument should be outlined. If, at the time of writing the proposal, the instrument is not yet developed, describe the step-by-step procedure that will be used to devise and pretest the instrument. In such cases indicate at least the categories or types of data that will be sought. Be sure these are explained in a way consistent with the definitions of the concepts and variables involved in the study and are explicitly linked to the study's objectives.

The validity, reliability, relevance, and sensitivity issues involved in each measuring device should be discussed. While social research measurement devices may not fully meet these criteria, it is valuable to demonstrate to the funder your awareness of the issues and limitations of these measures and of the extent of error that can be expected.

DATA COLLECTION PROCEDURES

Having described the kinds of data to be collected, the next step is to describe the step-by-step procedures that will be employed to collect the data. This provides the reader with a picture of what the researchers will actually be doing. Depending on the particular type of study, some examples of the material to cover here include:

- How tests will be administered
- What kinds of interviews will be held, what procedures interviewers will use, how appointments will be made, how respondent cooperation will be assured, how interviews will be recorded
- What books, records, files, or documents will be reviewed, how they will be obtained, how data will be extracted from them and by whom

- What procedures will be used in making field observations, how they will be recorded, who will conduct them
- How mail questionnaires will be sent out, what devices will be used for follow-up
- How will data be filed, what control mechanisms will be used, how errors and inconsistencies will be identified and corrected, what methods will be used to assure quality of data
- What supervisory methods will be used

The adequacy of the description of the research process demonstrates to the funder that the researchers know what tasks are involved and know how to do the work. It also documents the feasibility of the study and of the proposer's capability to successfully complete the project. It is especially important for new researchers without an established track record to provide a careful and complete presentation of this material. One should also check over this part of the proposal to be certain that it shows how expected obstacles (e.g., interviewer bias, failure to return mail questionnaires, lack of cooperation, unavailability of records) will be overcome.

In the case of studies that involve a considerable range of data and a number of different data sources, the use of a graphic data matrix can be an effective technique. The matrix can show (1) major data items listed vertically down the left side and (2) major data sources listed across the top. For each item of data the source(s) is checked off in the matrix. The use of the matrix technique serves a number of purposes. It provides the reader with a well-organized summary of the design. It also contributes to the coherency, internal consistency, and impact of the proposal.

DATA ANALYSIS

One of the major factors that can affect the success or failure of a proposal is the adequacy of the plan for analysis and interpretation of the data. This section of the proposal should cover a number of the following items:

How data will be assembled, coded, processed, edited, filed, and collated

What use of computers or other hardware will be involved

How data will be categorized and aggregated

What statistical methods will be used to obtain descriptive and inferential data and to identify relationships among variables

What kinds of charts and graphs will be used: pie charts, bar charts, line charts, scattergrams (includes dummy tables and charts that are expected to result from the analysis)

What will be the basis for the interpretation of the data and/or hypothesis testing

How the data analysis will be related to all of the study objectives

What step-by-step tasks and procedures will be employed in the data analysis phase of the study

FINAL REPORT

Include an outline of the organization of the final research report in the proposal. The more specific the outline, the more the proposal will be strengthened. At a minimum all research reports should cover the following major topics:

A. An Abstract
B. Introduction
C. Problem Statement
D. Study Procedures
E. Findings and Conclusions
F. Appendixes

This basic outline can be expanded by adding as many subheadings as possible. While these will depend largely on the particular problem and research methodology, a number of general areas can be anticipated, as shown in the following outline:

A. Abstract or Summary of Method, Findings, and Conclusions
B. Introduction
   1. Purpose of the Study
   2. Study Objectives or Hypotheses
   3. Overall Research Approach
   4. Organization of the Report

C. Problem Statement
  1. Nature and Extent of the Problem
  2. Significance
  3. Conceptual Model and Definitions
  4. Related Literature Review
D. Study Procedures
  1. Overall Design
  2. Discussion of Variables and Operational Definitions
  3. Description of Data Sources
  4. Data Collection Methods
    a. Instrumentation
    b. Procedures
  5. Data Analysis Techniques
E. Findings and Conclusions
  Outline the major areas of findings expected to emerge and the areas in which conclusions will be presented. Use the problem definition, specific questions, objectives, or hypothesis described earlier in the proposal as guides to identify these specific areas in this part of the proposal. Include dummy tables and charts expected to be included in final report.
F. Appendixes
  1. Sample Instruments
  2. Tables
  3. Other Background Information

WORK PLAN, PHASING, AND TIMETABLES

A step-by-step work plan and time schedule should be projected and described in the proposal. Each operation or task should be listed in as sequential a form as possible, including the starting and completion time for each activity. Use one of the charts or diagrams explained on page 61 in chapter 4 to make this section as clear as possible. In the case of federally funded projects where Office of Management and Budget (OMB) approval of instruments is required, include the anticipated time for this procedure. In addition, some agencies require that instruments and/or statements of the more detailed design be submitted to them for approval before the next phase of the study can begin. Show these steps in the work plan and timetable as well. If a period of time for review and approval by human subjects review committees is required, show this in the timetable. A recognition of these kinds of possible delays contributes to a more realistic work plan and to the credibility of the proposal writer's research expertise.

Be particularly careful in scheduling time for data collection activities, since these tasks are most frequently underestimated in planning research projects. Every procedure described in the earlier sections of the proposal must be accounted for in the work plan and timetables.

In complex projects, clarity can be added by grouping the tasks into three to five major phases of the study, such as those illustrated in the sample chart on page 54 in chapter 4.

ORGANIZATION AND PERSONNEL

As noted earlier, one of the major reasons for the failure of research proposals is that the reviewers are critical of either the qualifications of the proposed research staff or the organization of the staff. Experienced and established researchers, of course, do not have serious problems in this connection, but many proposal writers do not have a major performance record. Thus, the way this section of the proposal is presented can greatly strengthen the overall chances of success. One technique is to list each position. Begin with the project director or principal investigator followed by the rest of the staff positions. Briefly describe the job responsibilities and qualifications for each. Where it is known, briefly describe the competency (name, experience, and training) of the specific person who will be in the major positions. Attach a vitae as an appendix to the proposal for each person in a key position. Rather than use routine file vitaes, it is better to prepare individual vitaes geared to the specific purposes of the proposal so that the most relevant experience and training can be emphasized. In some cases, one may not have names of persons for all jobs. This omission is acceptable as long as the director/principal investigator and some top persons can be identified. Do not, however, include a specific individual's name and say "will be recruited if the project is funded." Make these arrangements before the proposal is submitted, or leave out the name.

Researchers without a track record can improve this section by including experienced persons as consultants and by stressing the overall research capability of the sponsoring institution or organization. When including consultants, be specific about their role and the tasks they will perform.

Explain how the staff will be structured and include an organizational chart as illustrated in chapter 4, showing lines of authority, communication, and supervision. Also indicate how the research unit will be related to the sponsoring institution. If committees or advisory groups are part of the plan, describe their composition, role, and relationships.

FACILITIES AND RESOURCES

Describe the capabilities of the institution sponsoring the research, and document the availability of the facilities and other resources necessary to carry out the project. List the specific facilities available, including the following if they are appropriate to the project:

- Office space and office equipment
- Field locations
- Computer resources
- Backup administrative and research staff support
- Library resources
- Filing and storage facilities
- Evidence of institutional commitment

Avoid using institutional "boiler-plate" descriptions. Instead, adapt them to the individual project.

BUDGET

The general guidelines for preparing the budget for a research proposal are the same as for other types of proposals, already presented in chapter 4, and are not repeated here.

Some aspects of budget preparation are especially applicable to research budgets, particularly when they are sponsored by academic institutions and when they are submitted to federal funding agencies. Most universities and colleges have research offices that establish the rules for budget presentation, cost sharing, and charging overhead (indirect expenses), and that assist researchers in this part of the task. One can expect that the application forms for most government research programs will call for more detail than foundations require.

7

MARKETING PROPOSALS

THIS CHAPTER DISCUSSES PRINCIPLES AND METHODS FOR IDENTIFYING, cultivating, and approaching funding sources in order to place your proposal in as favorable a position as possible. The chapter is titled "marketing proposals" rather than "selling proposals" because the methods suggested are based on marketing principles rather than those of sales. A marketing approach focuses on the management of the relationship between your organization and potential funding sources and makes use of methods such as market research, segmentation, positioning, and communicating with potential funders effectively. The marketing of proposals is seen as a competitive process in which the key to success is to produce a high-quality proposal that will be directed toward the most viable funding sources. The proposal marketplace is what is known as an "elastic market," that is, funders have a great deal of choice in what they may fund and are therefore very sensitive to variations in the quality, appeal, cost, and feasibility of the many proposals they receive.

From a marketing perspective the funder should be regarded as a consumer and the proposal seen as a product. A key principle of marketing is that consumer decisions are largely based on their assessment of five factors. First, is the product of high quality and does it offer the benefits the consumer is looking for? Second, is it readily accessible? Third, is it affordable? Fourth, is it appealing in terms of its appearance, color, and design? And, fifth, is the information received about the product persuasive?

Following the guidelines presented in earlier chapters can help assure that the proposal is of high quality and that its presentation is appealing, accessible (i.e., easy to read), and persuasive. But it is also necessary to know as much as possible about the potential funder's requirements and expectations, to direct the proposal to the funding sources where it will have the best chances of success, and, if necessary, to adapt the proposal in terms of style and presentation to conform more closely to the funder's style. This means that it is critical to develop a strategy to identify potential funders and to target the proposal so that it can be in the most advantageous competitive position. One of the ways this is accomplished is by engaging in market research as explained in the next section.

IDENTIFYING POTENTIAL FUNDERS

Identifying potential funders is the market research aspect of marketing a proposal. There are many published reports, books, directories, periodicals, newsletters, and commercial services that are available to help identify potential funding sources for your proposed program or research proposal. Many of these are very extensive and can also be expensive. Chapter 8 includes a list and description of some of the most useful of these resources. By far the most useful guide to identifying foundations is the latest edition of *The Foundation Directory*, published by The Foundation Center, 79 Fifth Avenue, New York, NY 10003; and, for identifying federal government programs, *The Catalog of Domestic Assistance*, available from the Superintendent of Documents, U.S. Government Printing Office, Washington, D.C. 20402. The search can be facilitated by using the computer search facilities of the Foundation Center and the computerized retrieval system known as the Federal Assistance Programs Retrieval System (FAPRS), which provides access to material in the *Catalog*. Both of these computer search resources are explained in chapter 8.

The first step in developing a marketing approach is to do some preliminary market planning, known as segmentation. Segmentation refers to the process of taking the market, in this case the universe of potential funders, and dividing it into a few key groups, or segments, each of which has similar characteristics. After you have completed writing the proposal, you can classify it according to certain characteristics and then limit yourself to funding sources that match those characteristics. The key factors in classifying the proposal include:

1. In what *geographic area* will the proposed activity take place? Many foundations only support programs in specific areas. The first step, therefore, is to identify only foundations that provide grants to organizations in your area.

2. What is the particular *field of service*, problem area, and target population characteristics that the proposal covers? Using the *Foundation Directory* one can identify foundations according to these factors since the *Directory* is cross-indexed in this manner.

3. What is the *size of the grant* being sought? A number of publications list the various grants made by each foundation, what organization received the grant and the amount of the grant. In this way, one can identify foundations that grant amounts similar to the amount you are requesting.

4. Is the *proposal* for regular operating expense, capital expense, a special project, research, or other funds? Various foundations limit the kinds of grants they make. These limitations are usually specified in the description of the foundation found in the *Directory* and similar publications.

Similar to the information on foundations, various publications provide this information for government programs. For example, *The Directory of Awards* of the National Science Foundation lists the grants made by the National Science Foundation. Publications of this kind also give one a sense of the extent of competition for grants. For example, in a recent year the National Science Foundation reported receiving a total of 5,554 proposals and funding a total of 1,637, meaning that a little less than one-third of the proposals it received were funded. In many foundations, only one out of every ten proposals may be funded in a given year.

Doing the kind of market research outlined here can be time consuming and many of the available publications and computer search services are expensive. Because of the very large number of potential funding sources and the highly competitive market, one needs to be as selective as possible. A lot of material must be reviewed and then one has to concentrate on the more promising possibilities. But, experience has shown that it pays off!

TARGETING AND POSITIONING THE PROPOSAL

After a list of potential foundation or government funders has been developed, the next step is to target the proposal so that it will be as attractive as possible to the funder. There are a number of different ways to obtain the information needed to ascertain whether you should rewrite some parts of the proposal for this purpose. While it is not suggested that one should change the basic ideas and approach that have been developed, it is often useful to consider revising some of the language in order to communicate with funders in the terms that they are familiar with and will best understand.

One way to do this is to obtain a copy of the annual report of the foundation, read it carefully and determine whether the proposal could be made more consistent with the style and content of the language used by the foundation.

Another way to make the proposal as specific as possible to any one particular funder is to make contact by phone or in person with a staff person at the foundation or government program to which you may send the proposal. Many proposal writers are hesitant to do this because they "don't have the time" or "feel intimidated." This is a major mistake. One should not hesitate to call and, if possible, make appointments with staff people. Remember, foundation staff and government officials are there to respond to public needs and demands. Most importantly, these staff people are rewarded by their success in effectively managing their part of the funder's grant program. They are interested in identifying and funding the best possible programs.

Staff people at foundations are relatively easy to locate just by calling the foundation office. Identifying the right person to talk to in a government funding program may take a little more work. The federal government has an office for just about everything. These agencies have staff people located in either their Washington offices or their regional offices who can help by telling you if they have a program suitable to fund the proposed activity. If they do, they can send you explanatory material, such as program announcements and guidelines, and can advise you regarding the appropriateness of your proposal for their funding program. If they do not have an appropriate program, suggestions regarding other possible programs can be requested. Very often one can get a very good lead to a possible funding source through these contacts.

Much of this part of marketing a proposal can be done on the telephone. It will save you time, and, because many foundations and government programs have quite small staffs, they do not have time for many personal visits. Do not hesitate to send the proposal to a number of different funders at the same time. This is perfectly ethical, and almost all funders expect that you will be doing this. It is also proper to attempt to obtain joint or partial support for the proposal from a number of different funding sources. One can be frank about this in dealing with funders. In some cases, the funder may take the initiative in arranging for joint financing or suggesting other more appropriate funding sources.

When submitting your proposal to multiple funders, a most important step in targeting the proposal is adapting it to each funder to whom it will be sent, the adapting process can be simplified by using word processing programs. The changes are usually only in a few paragraphs and require a minimum of work with the possibility of a considerable payoff. The letter of transmittal and the first paragraph of the proposal almost always must be revised since they contain the funder's name and reference to the funder's interests to which the proposal is responsive. In addition, if you see that the written material from the funder favors certain words or phrases, you may wish to use them in the proposal. For example, a foundation's program guidelines may repeatedly use the word "partnership." Your proposal may include activities aimed at developing "cooperative relationships" among agencies to implement a program activity. Consider using the word "partnership" to describe these relationships at some point in the proposal.

It is very important for agencies and organizations seeking foundation or government grants to be aware of the policies, procedures, and regulations that pertain to both the submission of the proposal and that govern the administration of the grant once it is received. Request all the written material that can be obtained from funders and take the time to read it carefully. The material will provide you with information to help give your proposal the competitive edge necessary to be successful in the funding marketplace.

One of the important issues involved in targeting proposals is whether you should try to build political support for the proposal, especially in the case of government funding programs. Experience has shown that in the long run this is almost always counterproductive. Senators, members of Congress local officials, and others can be very helpful in identifying potential funding sources and obtaining resource material regarding government programs, but their direct intervention is usually not appreciated by the funding staff. More appropriately, these officials may offer letters of support and cooperation that may be attached to the proposal rather than personally intervening. There are times when conflict and disagreement may be so serious between a funder and an applicant that such intervention is needed, but these occasions are very rare.

Another aspect of targeting a proposal is deciding how much support should be requested of any one individual funder. The range of possible support can usually be ascertained by:

1. Examining the written material from the foundation or government funder. Some funders have specific guidelines, ranges, and limits on the amount of support they provide.

2. Examining the amount granted by the funder to the various projects supported in the past. This material is available in the annual reports of foundations and in the various directories and publications listed in chapter 8.

3. Asking the appropriate person in the foundation or government agency for this information. Grant information is public information and your right to this information is protected by federal and state laws and regulations.

It is advisable to get on the mailing lists of foundations and the various federal and state agencies that provide funds in the fields of interest to your organization. In this way you can build your own resource library of helpful information. In requesting to be placed on a mailing list you can follow the federal guidelines for this purpose, which call for the following information:

- Name and address of your organization
- Type of organization and area of interest
- Names of officers
- Size of the organization
- Kinds of programs for which you seek grants or contracts

A great deal of information is available to help applicants be more successful in obtaining funds, but one must seek out the information.

GOVERNMENT MARKET OR FOUNDATION MARKET?

There are many similarities but also some significant differences between foundation funding and governmental funding for projects and research activities. For one thing, foundations provide funds in the form of grants whereas government agencies more frequently use contracts. A discussion of the differences between these two forms of providing funds was presented in chapter 2, "Types of Proposals."

GOVERNMENT MARKET

When preparing a proposal to government funding sources, keep in mind that there are five important factors that differentiate them from private foundations. First, proposals submitted to federal, state, county, city, town, or other local government agencies are requesting governmental or public (i.e., tax) funds to support a particular program. Governmental monies are expended under specific legislative appropriations and authorizations that are expressed in laws, acts, bills, or resolutions of the legislative body (for instance, Congress, state assembly, county supervisors, city council, and so on). These funds are only allocated through grants or contracts that are clearly within the legislative provisions that authorize their expenditure.

Second, in addition to the legislative authority to expend such funds, governmental funding agencies are guided by specific written rules, regulations, and written guidelines that govern the administration of each program. These are usually drawn up by the government department, agency, or unit responsible for administering the program. They have been subjected to public hearings and then revised and adopted by the department. They are public documents, which are available upon request. The *Federal Register* can be checked for these materials.

Third, governmental agencies, particularly federal agencies, also prepare and print pamphlets and reports that explain the philosophy and approach of various specific government programs. These are also available upon request.

Fourth, another aspect of governmental funding is referred to as "legislative intent." This refers to the intentions of the legislative body that established a particular program when it passed a bill. The intent is reflected in statements made by legislative committees when they report out bills for approval; it can be found in committee reports. As public administrators move to implement these programs, they are guided, in part, by their understanding of this intent.

Fifth, most public agencies require that budgets and often the entire proposal be submitted on forms that they have devised for this purpose. Taken together, the laws, rules, regulations, guidelines, forms, programmatic reports, and programmatic philosophies establish the limits, priorities, and ground rules for making decisions about the allocation of public funds by governmental bodies. By studying them carefully one can assure that the proposal is responsive to and within the limits of what the public agency can legally support.

FOUNDATION MARKET

Foundations are influenced in their funding decisions by a set of factors, some of which are similar and some of which are different from those that influence governmental funders. First, each foundation is incorporated as a nonprofit organization and, as such, has a set of general purposes and policies that establishes the general nature and limitations on the kind of projects it may support. These purposes and policies sometimes represent the conditions set forth by the original donor(s) who established the foundation. In other cases they are established by the officers or board of directors of the foundation. Limits may be set by foundations on:

- The type of program to be supported
- The geographical area within which the foundation may support programs
- The minimum or maximum amount that can be granted to any applicant
- The type of organization that can receive grants

Since passage of the Federal Tax Reform Act and various state legislation, foundations have become more cautious in their procedures and generally prefer to make grants only to incorporated nonprofit organizations. The Internal Revenue Service issues "letters of exemption" to groups, organizations, and agencies that conduct nonprofit operations. These letters, which are obtained through formal application to the Internal Revenue Service, serve to assure the foundation that the applying organization can legitimately receive foundation grants without imposing liability on the foundation. If the organization does not have an exemption letter, it is sometimes possible to have the proposed project sponsored by a larger established agency whose charitable, religious, or educational nonprofit status is already established and whose purposes are similar to those set forth in the proposal.

Final decisions or ratification with respect to grants are generally made by the foundation board or committees, based on review of the proposal by the foundation's paid staff members. In large foundations there may be a number of levels of staff review. (In the case of government agencies, there are almost always at least two levels of staff review and the final decision is made by top bureau, unit, or departmental officials. In addition, many government agencies will sometimes utilize review panels of expert consultants as part of their review and decision-making process.)

Foundations range from those that have a wide range of general purposes to those that have very specialized interests. In general, the larger the foundation, the wider its range of interests. By reviewing the *Foundation Directory*, requesting copies of the foundation's annual report of its grant support, and talking to others who are experienced in proposal writing and seeking foundation support, one can ascertain which foundations may be interested in the subject of the proposal. Selectivity is advised. There are more than 27,000 foundations, many quite small, and it is certainly not feasible to review all of them.

Support may be sought from more than one foundation at the same time, or, from both governmental and foundation sources at the same time. It is not unusual for promising projects in the human service field to obtain support from both these sources.

Corporations and corporate foundations also have special interests. Large corporate foundations operate much like other foundations. Corporate foundations are particularly interested in supporting projects that will reflect well on the reputation of the corporation. They also have a special interest in projects that will improve the quality of life in the communities in which they are located.

Keep in mind that both the government and foundations have funds that they *must* spend. Although funders may appear to be hard-nosed and resistant, and although there is considerable competition for the same dollars, there is still pressure on the funders to locate and support promising and credible programs.

Many foundations, whether they be large and of national scope or smaller ones that focus on supporting programs in their local community or state, prefer to support new programs and shy away from ongoing support for already established programs. This means that the proposal should clearly delineate the aspects of the proposed program or research that are innovative, new, and of a pilot or demonstration nature. It also means that the proposal should indicate concrete plans for continuation of the project after a period of foundation support.

Governmental agencies are prone to avoid supporting ongoing programs as well, but not to the extent that this characterizes foundations; and, of course, many government programs are for ongoing support of specific activities as authorized by law. Government funders, more than foundations, are also constrained by the provisions of the formal guidelines and regulations that govern each program. A proposal to a governmental source should be responsive to these guidelines. Some foundations have also established certain priorities and program emphases that define more specifically than their statements of purpose the kinds of projects they are interested in supporting. However, they often have more flexibility than most government agencies in their pattern of support. This does not necessarily mean that foundations are always the principal supporters of innovation, demonstration, and experimentation. Actually, sometimes governmental agencies play this role, and at other times foundations do.

In addition to foundations, corporations, and government agencies, other possible sources of support should not be overlooked, such as labor unions, certain church groups, and community organizations and associations. These do not present major possibilities, since they usually have limited resources. On a local basis, however, they may open possibilities for partial support of a proposed project.

APPEALING TO FUNDER INTERESTS

A number of different types of interests may appeal to governmental funding agencies or foundations, including:

1. *Problem solutions.* Support of programs aimed at alleviating, reducing, or preventing particular social problems such as delinquency, family breakdown, mental illness, dependency, nutritional deficiencies, waste of resources, group conflict, and so on.

2. *Methodological demonstrations.* Support of programs that will demonstrate, test, or assess particular strategies, methods,

and techniques for solving problems, serving people, evaluating and managing programs, and so on.

3. *Institution building.* Support to improve, extend, or strengthen existing agencies and organizations such as schools, orchestras, libraries, hospitals, and so on.

4. *Individual achievement.* Support to individuals to carry out individual work that shows intellectual, cultural, scholarly, or artistic promise; or, to enable individuals to pursue further training in professional fields.

5. *Social-value contributions.* Support for projects or work that has or may have intrinsic social value and benefit to society in general, such as basic research and education.

The fact that all these types of projects may be of interest to both governmental agencies and foundations serves to illustrate that any specific project may be suitable for support from either one of these sources. Both may be tried if the government program and foundation within whose scope of interest the program may fall can be located. Foundations and government agencies are so numerous and diverse that it is impossible to make more specific categorical statements that apply to all of them. Only research and experience can provide the specific information required to successfully pursue the funding sources most likely to respond to a proposal.

PACKAGING THE PROPOSAL

As noted at the beginning of this chapter, the appearance of the proposal is one of the factors that will influence how a funder reacts to the material. While some funders may state in their guidelines that they are "interested in content, not form," research has shown that written material presented in different formats can evoke more or less favorable responses from readers. This is true because a part of how we respond to visual stimuli is based on emotional and physiological responses over which we have little control. In addition, we all have been socialized into attaching certain meanings to different shapes and colors. Some simple examples can illustrate these principles. The color red has a meaning that we don't consciously have to think about—"stop." If people are shown an arrow and a circle and asked to match the words "direction" and "unity" to these shapes, practically everyone will associate direction with an arrow and unity with a circle.*

In a way it is helpful to think of the appearance of the proposal as a figurative representation of your organization and a projection of its image. Attractive, well organized, nicely balanced, easy to look at, neat and uncluttered, attention getting but not showy; these are the visual qualities that one wants to project. Here are some guidelines for improving the proposal's appearance and its impact on the reader:

- Always use white—not colored—8½-by-11-inch paper

- Be sure that all pages are numbered

- Be sure that all tables and figures are numbered

- Leave adequate margins: no less than 1 inch on the sides, top, and bottom

- Use frequent headings and subheadings as explained on page 32

- Send the proposal in a large envelope so that it does not have to be folded

- Make sure the copy has been proofread by someone other than the person(s) who wrote it

- Include one or two charts such as an organization chart, bar chart, Gantt chart, or flowchart as explained in chapter 4**

*For a full explanation of the relationship between form and the processing of information see Robert Lefferts, *How to Prepare Charts and Graphs for Effective Reports* (New York: Harper & Row, 1982).

**An easy-to-follow guide for the preparation of charts and graphs can be found in Robert Lefferts, *How to Prepare Charts and Graphs for Effective Reports* (New York: Harper & Row, 1982). One of the most helpful tools to use in preparing charts and diagrams is a plastic template available from most office-supply stores. There are hundreds of different templates. Those with the most useful set of symbols such as rectangles, arrows, and circles are the computer diagrammers and organization chart templates manufactured by a number of companies.

- Use standard type styles and avoid italic or other scriptlike typefaces
- Do not use plastic binders and covers. Attach pages with paper clips or a single staple so the pages can be removed easily for duplicating
- Do not use a justified (i.e., flush) right-hand margin unless you have the capability to assure proportional spacing so that there is no distracting uneven spaces between words
- Single-space the narrative unless the funder specifies otherwise
- If your computer printer cannot produce letter-quality copy, borrow someone's. Light, difficult-to-read computer copy should never be sent to a funder
- Do not use abbreviations or etceteras
- Do not decorate the cover or pages with the border designs and other graphics you might have available on your computer program

WRITING STYLE

A decision always must be made regarding the writing style that will be employed, particularly whether to write in a personal or institutional style. A personal style is one in which personal references are made in the first person or third person such as:

> We are submitting our proposal to develop a new program based on our experience in our agency.

An institutional style would read:

> The proposal to develop a new program is based on the organization's experience in this field over the past two years.

There is no hard-and-fast rule to follow in selecting between these two writing styles. Avoid overpersonalizing the writing style of a proposal by avoiding words such as "I," "you," and "my." Third-person words such as "we" and "our" are somewhat more impersonal and many proposal writers like to use them. Be careful not to identify the concepts and methods being presented in the proposal with personal as compared to institutional ideas and experiences, since this can detract from the general importance and applicability of what is being proposed. (The exception to this, of course, would be in the case of grants sought by individuals rather than organizations.)

A review of the reports of a number of foundations reveals variation in usage among foundations. For example, some foundations write, "We accept proposals. . . ." while others write "The foundation accepts proposals. . . ." By and large, however, the primary style among foundations is more institutional than personal. This suggests using a mixed style in the proposal with an emphasis on the institutional approach.

The final style issue concerns the use of examples and quotations. Many readers tend to skip over what they consider to be "long" case examples and quotations. What is "long?" Examples and quotations that exceed five or six lines tend to be scanned rather than read, unless there is a high degree of interest in the item. Funders want to hear your ideas and they want to hear them in your own language.

8

RESOURCES FOR
LOCATING FUNDING
SOURCES AND
PREPARING PROPOSALS

THIS CHAPTER DESCRIBES SOME OF THE MORE HELPFUL RESOURCES THAT proposal writers can use to locate promising funding sources and prepare their proposals.

In recent years there has been a literal boom in the number of books, directories, periodicals, newsletters, and computer-aided searches available to proposal writers as they seek to identify potential funding sources for their proposals. Some of these resources are very useful. Some promise more than they deliver. Most are quite expensive. None will do the job by themselves. There is no magic formula for identifying a promising funding source other than a lot of hard work. Because there are so many different funding sources and so many different resources to use, it takes a good deal of time to review them and to follow up on the information obtained. Due to this proliferation of materials, it is necessary to use them as selectively as possible.

Following is a guide to some of the most widely used resources and those that are particularly helpful in the human services field.

FOUNDATION FUNDING

The Foundation Center is the number one resource for obtaining information on foundations through its various publications and the services of the Foundation Center Library. Rightly calling itself "The Nation's Most Authoritative Source of Information on Foundation & Corporate Philanthropy," the Center operates an extensive network of libraries that are open to the public. Its main reference sources are at its New York City headquarters and its three other reference collections in Washington, D.C., Cleveland, and San Francisco. In addition, the Center has cooperating libraries throughout the country, a list of which appears in Appendix B. The four reference collections are located at:

The Foundation Center
79 Fifth Avenue
New York, NY 10003
212-620-4230 or
1-800-424-9836

The Foundation Center
1001 Connecticut Avenue, N.W.
Washington, DC 20036
202-331-1400

The Foundation Center
312 Sutter Street
San Francisco, CA 94108
415-397-0902

The Foundation Center
Kent H. Smith Library
1422 Euclid Avenue
Cleveland, OH 44115
216-861-1933

Three of the most useful publications of the Center include:

• *The Foundation Directory.* Get the latest edition. The 12th edition was available in 1990 at a cost of $115 for paper and $135 for hardbound.

The *Directory* is the best up-to-date reference guide to major foundations. Contains information on more than 6,600 foundations awarding $6 billion in grants annually. Lists foundations with assets of $1 million or more and awarding $100,000 a year or more. Listings are indexed according to fields of interest and geography. A sample of the material found in the *Directory* is shown in Figure 13.

• *National Data Book of Foundations: A Comprehensive Guide to Grantmaking Foundations, 13th edition, 1989.* (2 Volumes) $75.

This book is the most complete guide to foundation giving that you could ask for. With briefer entries than the *Directory*, the *Data Book* lists more than 27,000 foundations filing with the Internal Revenue Service. Gives names of foundations, amounts granted, address, and contact person. Geographic listing helps locate local foundations and community foundations that may only make grants in particular localities. Includes a bibliography of directories of state and local foundations (This bibliography is shown in Appendix C).

• *The Foundation Grants Index*, 18th edition, 1989. $65.

Many proposal writers like this publication because it actually describes more than 43,000 grants made by 400 or so foundations. It tells you who received each grant and what the project was. An excellent way to determine what kind of projects a foundation supports and the amount of money it grants for individual projects. Also published is the *Foundation Grants Index Bimonthly*, which lists recent grants as an update to those in the *Grants Index*. Six issues, $36.

Other publications and services of the Foundation Center include:

• *Corporate Foundation Profiles*, 5th edition, 1988. $75.

Provides information on 771 of the major corporate foundations indexed according to fields of interest, geography, and types of support. For the price, one of the best guides to corporate resources.

• *National Directory of Corporate Giving*, 1989. $175.

Lists more than 1,500 U.S. corporations with annual sales of $200 million or more including address, subsidiaries, foundations, giving pattern, and application information. The corporate field can change rapidly, so be sure to contact companies for up-to-date information.

• *Foundation Grants to Individuals*, 6th edition, 1988. $24.

A comprehensive source for information about funding sources that will support individual (as compared to organizational) projects. Organized by type of activity that will be supported and explains limitations of various funders in supporting individual applications.

• *Comsearch*

A series of printouts targeted to four general areas and providing specific information within each area, as follows:

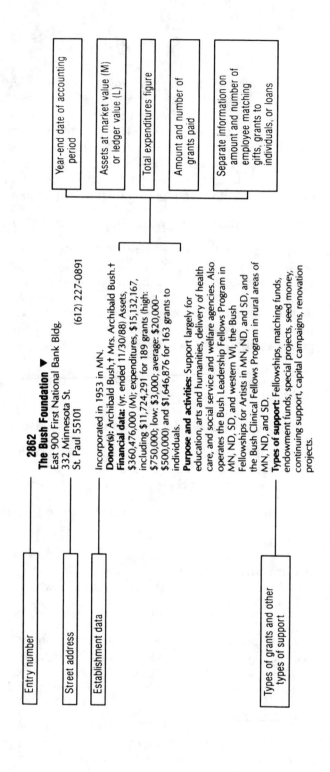

Entry number

Street address

Establishment data

Types of grants and other types of support

Year-end date of accounting period

Assets at market value (M) or ledger value (L)

Total expenditures figure

Amount and number of grants paid

Separate information on amount and number of employee matching gifts, grants to individuals, or loans

2862
The Bush Foundation ▼
East 900 First National Bank Bldg.
332 Minnesota St.
St. Paul 55101   (612) 227-0891

Incorporated in 1953 in MN.
Donor(s): Archibald Bush,† Mrs. Archibald Bush.†
Financial data: (yr. ended 11/30/88) Assets, $360,476,000 (M); expenditures, $15,132,167, including $11,724,291 for 189 grants (high: $750,000; low: $3,000; average: $20,000–$500,000) and $1,646,876 for 163 grants to individuals.

Purpose and activities: Support largely for education, arts and humanities, delivery of health care, and social service and welfare agencies. Also operates the Bush Leadership Fellows Program in MN, ND, SD, and western WI, the Bush Fellowships for Artists in MN, ND, and SD, and the Bush Clinical Fellows Program in rural areas of MN, ND, and SD.

Types of support: Fellowships, matching funds, endowment funds, special projects, seed money, continuing support, capital campaigns, renovation projects.

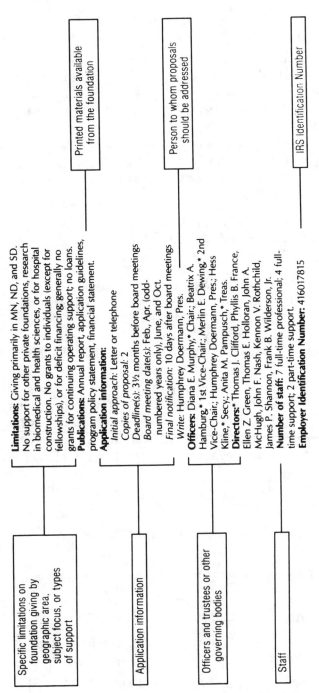

Figure 13. Sample entry from *The Foundation Directory.*

Reprinted with permission from *The Foundation Directory,* Edition 12, the Foundation Center, New York, NY, 1989.

Comsearch: Broad Topics. Each printout covers a topical area such as crime, family services, film, women, and the like. Shows each grant of $5,000 or more in the topical area including name of foundation, name and location of recipient, and data on the foundation. $45 for each topical report.

Comsearch: Subjects. Each printout covers information on foundations and grants organized according to 26 different subjects such as homeless, mental health, rural development and the like. $25 for each subject.

Comsearch: Geographics. Lists foundation grants for various geographic areas including New York City, Washington, D.C., 11 large states, and 7 regions. $45 each.

Comsearch: Special Topics. These printouts can be ordered to obtain information that lists foundations by the size of the assets, total giving, or other characteristics. $25 each.

The Center's various data bases are all computerized and can be accessed from home or office. Information can be obtained from the Center at 212-620-4230 and data bases can be assessed through DIALOG (415-858-2700) or the Telecommunications Cooperative Network (212-714-9780). The Center also has an Associates Program, which entitles the member to access the Center's services by phone. Basic annual membership charge is $375.

The Center also publishes a number of guides to funding resources in special fields. These include:

• *National Guide to Foundation Funding in Health,* 1988. $95.

Lists more than 2,500 health funders as well as their programs and policies.

• *Alcohol and Drug Abuse Funding,* 1989. $40.

A study of private, corporate, and community foundation funding for alcohol and drug abuse programs in the 1980s.

• *Grants for Arts and Cultural Programs,* 1990. $105.

Lists 6,000 grants by more than 370 foundations for arts and cultural programs.

• *National Guide to Funding in Aging,* 1987. $35.

Covers federal, state, and foundation sources for funds to support programs for older people.

• *AIDS Funding*, 1988. $35.

A guide to giving by foundations and charitable organizations that have supported AIDS-related programs listing the interests and limitations of these funders as well as information on the AIDS grants that were awarded. A companion publication is:

Meeting the Challenge: Foundation Response to AIDS. Reports on interviews with foundation leaders regarding support for AIDS programs.

The Center issues a periodic publication catalog, which you can obtain by calling the Center in New York City. The catalog lists about 25 books of interest that the Center distributes. These include:

• *New York State Foundations: A Comprehensive Directory*, 1988. $150.

• *The State and the Voluntary Sector: A Report of New York State Project 2000*, 1988. $14.95.

• *Foundations Today: 6th Edition*, 1989. $9.50.

• *The Nonprofit Entrepreneur: Creating Ventures to Earn Income*, edited by Edward Skloot, 1988. $19.95.

• *Securing Your Organization's Future: A Complete Guide to Fundraising Strategies*, Michael Seltzer, 1987. $24.95.

• *Managing for Profit in the Nonprofit World*, Paul B. Firstenberg, 1986. $19.95.

• *Promoting Issues & Ideas: A Guide to Public Relations for Nonprofit Organizations*, Public Interest Public Relations Inc., 1987. $19.95.

• *The Board Member's Book*, Brian O'Connell, 1985. $16.95.

• *Foundation Fundamentals: A Guide for Grantseekers*, 3rd edition, Patricia E. Read, 1986. $9.95.

• *The Literature of the Nonprofit Sector: A Bibliography with Abstracts*, 1989. $50.

The Center has an annual subscription service ($295) to its *Source Book Profiles,* which is published over a two-year cycle. Each cycle covers 500 foundations and provides comprehensive information on the foundation.

FEDERAL FUNDING

The best single resource for leads on federal funding programs is published by the federal government and is called the *Catalog of Federal Domestic Assistance.* Over the years a number of bills have been introduced in the U.S. Congress to improve the accessibility of information about federal funding programs. The Federal Program Information Act, passed in 1977 and then amended in 1984, provides the legislative mandate for the publishing of the *Catalog* and its computerized version, known as the Federal Assistance Programs Retrieval System (FAPRS).

• *Catalog of Federal Domestic Assistance,* Superintendent of Documents, U.S. Government Printing Office, Washington, DC 20402. $38. Order latest edition.

A 1,000-plus page manual that lists federal assistance and grant programs cross-indexed by agency and program types. For each program, information is provided on its name, location in the federal maze of agencies, program objectives, eligibility requirements, application and approval process, who to contact, examples of funded programs, and criteria for selecting proposals. Some of the directory information can become outdated quickly and not all descriptions are uniformly informative, Nevertheless, this catalog provides the best start in the search for federal funds. Figure 14 shows an excerpt from the *Catalog.*

• *Federal Assistance Program Retrieval System.*

This computer-based information program of federal grant programs mirrors the information in the *Catalog.* For information on the program, how to access it, and a list of access points serving your community, contact the Federal Domestic Assistance Catalog Staff, General Services Administration, Ground Floor, Reporter's Building, 300 7th St., S.W., Washington, DC 20407. The telephone is 202-453-4126.

13.151 PROJECT GRANTS FOR HEALTH SERVICES TO THE HOMELESS

(Homeless Assistance Program)

FEDERAL AGENCY: BUREAU OF HEALTH CARE DELIVERY AND ASSISTANCE, HEALTH RESOURCES AND SERVICES ADMINISTRATION, PUBLIC HEALTH SERVICE, DEPARTMENT OF HEALTH AND HUMAN SERVICES

AUTHORIZATION: Public Health Service Act, Section 340, as amended; Stewart B. McKinney Homeless Assistance Act of 1987, as amended, Public Law 100-77.

OBJECTIVES: To provide health care services to homeless persons. A homeless individual is defined as one who lacks housing, including persons in emergency shelters or in transitional housing.

TYPES OF ASSISTANCE: Project grants.

USES AND USE RESTRICTIONS: Grant funds can be used to provide: (1) primary care services; (2) substance abuse services; (3) 24-hour emergency services, including mental health service referrals; and (4) a system for impatient referrals, outreach, and aid in establishing eligibility for appropriate entitlement programs. Grants will be awarded only to pubic or nonprofit entities. Grant funds may not be expended for : (1) impatient care, except for treatment of substance abuse provided in settings other than hospitals; (2) cash payments to recipients; (3) purchase or improvement of real property (other than minor remodeling); or (4) purchase of major medical equipment (except if waived by the Secretary for Health and Human Services under the provisions of the statute). Federal funds may not supplant existing public or private resources that are currently allocated to assist homeless populations. Under section 340(e), Federal funds may not exceed 75 percent of the costs of services under the grant. Not more than 10 percent of grant funds may be spent for administrative costs.

ELIGIBILITY REQUIREMENTS:

Applicant Eligibility: Public or private nonprofit institutions or organizations, State and local governments, Federally-Recognized Indian Tribal Governments, and U.S. Territories and Possessions.

Beneficiary Eligibility: Homeless individuals with special emphasis given to elderly persons, handicapped persons, families with children, Native Americans, and veterans.

Credentials/Documentation: Costs will be determined in accordance with 45 CFR, Part 74, Subpart Q, for nonprofit organizations and OMB Circular No. A–87, "Cost Principles for State and Local Governments."

APPLICATION AND AWARD PROCESS:

Preapplication Coordination: Informal inquires regarding the program and intent to submit an application should be directed to the appropriate Public Health Service (PHS) Regional Health Administrator. (See Appendix IV of the Catalog for listing of locations.) The application package will be made available by the Department « Health and Human Services (DHHS) (Form PHS-5161-1, with revised factsheet, DHHS-424). The application kit contains a list of States which have been chosen to set up a review system and will provide a point of contact in the state for that review. This program is eligible for coverage under E.O. 12372, "Intergovernmental Review of Federal Programs." An applicant should consult the office or officials designated as the single point of contact in his or her State for more information on the process the State requires to be followed in applying for assistance, if the State has selected the program for review. The standard application forms, as furnished by DHHS and required by 45 CFR, 92 must be used for this program.

Application Procedure: Application is made by the submission of DHHS Application, Form PHS-5161-1. Applications may be obtained by writing to the appropriate DHHS Regional Health Administrator. (See Appendix IV of the Catalog for listing of locations.) Applicants must submit a written commitments of active support and contribution of local resources including a description of the 25 percent nonfederal contribution and must contain assurances required by statute. Applicants are subject to 45 CFR, Part 92 and OMB Circular No. A-110, "Grants and Agreements with Institutes of Higher Education, Hospitals and Other Nonprofit Organizations."

Award Procedure: Applications will be reviewed by a committee composed of DHHS staff members. Applications are reviewed for merit and are recommended for approval or disapproval. Grant awards will be made by the appropriate Regional Health Administrator.

Deadlines: Future deadlines information will be specified in the application instructions. Contact the appropriate DHHS Regional Health Administrator for further information. (See Appendix IV of the Catalog for locations.)

Range of Approval/Disapproval Time: Approximately 60 days.

Appeals: None.

Renewals: Support is recommended for a specified project period. not in excess of 2 years. After initial awards are made, continuation projects will be reviewed annually and funded if approved.

ASSISTANCE CONSIDERATIONS:

Formula and Matching Requirements: Applications must have a written plan and commitment of active support and contribution of local resources including at least a 25 percent nonfederal contribution for the provision of health care services. Nonfederal contributions may be in cash or in-kind, fairly evaluated, including plants, equipment, or services.

Length and Time Phasing of Assistance: Awards are made annually. After funds are issued, funds are released in accordance with payment procedures of DHHS, which may be an Electronic Transfer System or a monthly cash request system.

POST ASSISTANCE REQUIREMENTS:

Reports: Grantees will be required to submit reports semi-annually on the quantity, type, and cost of services provided to homeless individuals. Reports will follow Bureau Commmon Reporting Requirements (BCRR). Annual progress and financial status reports are required at the end of each budget period and final reports must be submitted at the end of the project period.

Audits: Programs will follow the guidelines cited in OMB Circular No. A-110, "Grant and Agreements with Institutions of Higher Education, Hospitals, and Other Nonprofit Organizations," and OMB Circular No. A-128, "Audits of State and Local Governments." In accordance with the provisions of OMB Circular No. A-128, "Audits of State and Local Governments," State and local governments that receive financial assistance of $100,000 or more within the State's fiscal year shall have an audit mad for that year. State and local governments that receive between $25,000 and $100,000 within the State's fiscal year shall have an audit made in accordance with Circular No. A-128, or in accordance Federal laws and regulations governing the programs in which they participate.

Records: Financial records must be kept available for 3 years after submission of expenditure reports and 3 years after final disposition of non-expendable property. If questions remain such as those raised as a result of an audit, records must be retained until the problem is resolved.

FINANCIAL INFORMATION:

Account Identification: 79-0330-0-2-331

Obligations: (Grants) FY 88 $14,232,390; FY 89 est $14,820,000; and FY 90 est $63,600,000.

Range and Average of Financial Assistance: $62,000 to $2,000,000; $285,000.

PROGRAM ACCOMPLISHMENTS: There were 109 grants awarded from fiscal year 1988 funds to 109 public and private non-profit entities in 43 States, the District of Columbia, and Puerto Rico. The 109 projects provide health care services to approximately 400,000 homeless persons. In fiscal year 1989, the $14.8 million appropriated will be limited to continuation awards of grantees funded in fiscal year 1988. In the fiscal year 1990, it is anticipated that approximately 53 grants will be awarded.

REGULATIONS, GUIDELINES, AND LITERATURE: Pertinent information is contained in the 52 CFR 32347, "Availability of Funds for Project Grants for Health Services to the Homeless Population," Section 340, Public Health Service Act, as amended by the Stewart B. McKinney Homeless Assistance Act, Public law 100-77, and the PHS Grants Policy Statement, DHHS Publication No. (OASH) 82-50,000 (Rev.), dated January 1, 1987.

INFORMATION CONTACTS:
Regional or Local Office: Regional Grant Management Officers of the appropriate DHHS Regional Offices. (See Appendix IV of the Catalog for a listing of Regional Offices.)
Headquarters Office: Harold Dame, Director, Health Care Services for the Homeless Program, Bureau for Health @re Delivery and Assistance, Health Resources and Services Administration, Room 7-15, Parklawn Building, 5600 Filshers Lane, Rockville, MD 10857. Telephone (301) 443-8134. (Use same 7-digit number for FTS.) Contact: Ms. Opal McCarthy, Grants Management Officer, BHCDA, Room 8A-17, Parklawn Building, 5600 Fishers Lane, Rockville, MD 20857. Telephone: (301) 443-3476. (Use same 7-digit number for FTS.)

RELATED PROGRAMS: 13,224, Community Health Centers; 13,258, National Health Service Corps.

EXAMPLES OF FUNDED PROJECTS: A Community Health Center formed a coalition of community representations and providers for the provision of the primary health care services, substance abuse, and mental health services to homeless individuals. Health care provider teams will reach out and travel to areas with heavy concentrations of homeless individuals. Homeless persons will be provided with health care outpatient services either at community health centers or in off-site locations, such as shelters for the homeless. The community health center will arrange for impatient services if required. Substance abuse services and mental health services will be contracted out to existing facilities within the community. The community coalition of providers represents organizations responsible for the provision of other homeless individual services such as: food, clothing and shelter. Through a system of case management, the community health center will serve to guide homeless persons to these services. A 24-hour emergency service has been arranged through a community hospital.

CRITERIA FOR SELECTING PROPOSALS: Grants awards will be based upon the following criteria: (1) the extent of the documented number of homeless persons to be serviced by the project; (2) the adequacy of the applicant's proposed delivery system for mental health services available and accessible to the homeless population; (3) the extent to which the applicant has commitments for active participation from health care providers; (4) the qualifications and experience of proposed staff; and (5) the adequacy of the proposed budget and the proposed plans for continuation without Federal support after the project period.

Figure 14. Sample entry from the *Catalog of Federal Domestic Assistance.* From *Elements of Graphics,* 1981, by Robert Lefferts. Reprinted by permission of Harper & Row, Publishers, Inc., New York.

• *Federal Register*, published five days a week. Superintendent of Documents, Government Printing Office, Washington, DC 20402. $170 for six months or $340 a year.

Reports on guidelines, rules, and regulations for many government programs.

• *Commerce Business Daily*, U.S. Department of Commerce, Superintendent of Documents, Government Printing Office Washington, DC 20402. $261.

Daily listing of government procurements, potential contracts, and awards.

• *United States Government Manual*, Superintendent of Documents, U.S. Government Printing Office, Washington, DC 20402. $20. Revised annually.

A listing of all federal departments and agencies including addresses, phone numbers, and principal officials.

Another source for information on government funding possibilities at the state level is from the state legislature. For example, in New York State the Speaker's Office puts out a monthly *Grants Action Newsletter* that provides information on grant programs available from state and federal agencies.

GENERAL INFORMATION

Some of the best sources of general information to assist proposal writers include:

The Grantsmanship Center
650 S. Spring St.
Suite 507
Los Angeles
CA 90014
213-689-9222
1-800-421-9512

Since its founding in 1972 The Grantsmanship Center has become the leading training organization for nonprofit organizations in relationship to proposal writing, fund-raising, and more recently, management. In addition to its extensive training programs, the Center has a number of fine publications, most of which are reprints of articles from its former publication, *The Granstmanship News*. The News has been replaced by a free publication that appears periodically known as *The Whole Nonprofit Catalog*. The *Catalog* not only includes information about the Center's programs but has articles on timely topics related to management and program planning and development. It also includes excellent information on new and useful publications for proposal writers. The Center's two most popular publications are:

• *Program Planning & Proposal Writing*, by the Center's director Norton J. Kiritz.

These are two booklets, one eight pages long and the other an expanded version, which is forty-eight pages long, which discuss the various elements of a proposal. Especially useful for human service projects, the booklets explain what to cover and how to present an introduction, needs assessment, objectives, program, evaluation, and budget. The eight-page booklet is $3.00; the 48-page booklet is $4.00. Order from The Grantsmanship Center, 650 S. Spring St., Suite 507, Box 6210, Los Angeles, CA 90014. (Add $2.00 for shipping.)

• *The Grantsmanship Book.*

A collection of reprints of articles published by the Center on grantsmanship, management, personnel and the like geared to the needs of nonprofits in the human service field. $59.95 plus $3.00 shipping from The Grantsmanship Center. For $21.95 (plus $2.50 shipping) you can get a package of nine articles (including the 48-page booklet) covering only proposal writing and grantsmanship.

Another excellent source of general information is:

• *The Chronicle of Philanthropy*, P.O. Box 1989, Marion, OH 43305. $57.50 year.

This biweekly (except for two weeks in August and December) came upon the scene in 1989 and quickly became the outstanding tabloid in the grants field. It includes up-to-date news of the nonprofit field, lists new grants given by selected foundations, lists coming events in the field, includes a directory of services, classified ads, and much more of interest to anyone in the world of philanthropy. Editorial offices are at 1255 Twenty-third Street, N.W., Washington, DC 20037.

A good general introduction to the funding field is:

• *Getting Funded: A Complete Guide to Proposal Writing*, by Mary Hall. Published by Continuing Education Publications, Portland State University, P.O. Box 1394, Portland, OR 97207. 1988. $19.95.

This book represents the third edition of what was called *Developing Skills in Proposal Writing*. It is a comprehensive explanation of the proposal writing process with many good examples. Full of checklists and detailed guidelines. Geared mostly, but not exclusively, to universities and research proposals, it is a worthwhile addition to a proposal writer's library.

RESEARCH PROPOSALS AND RESEARCH GRANTS

The following are among the materials helpful in preparing research proposals and identifying funding resources for research projects in the human service and behavioral science fields.

• *How to Prepare a Research Proposal: Guidelines for Funding Dissertations in the Social and Behavioral Sciences*, 3rd edition, David R. Krathwol, 1988, Syracuse University Press, Syracuse, NY 13210. $14.95.

One of the most widely used guides to preparing research proposals in the behavioral science area, it is aimed primarily at graduate students but contains helpful guidelines for preparing all types of research proposals.

• *Directory of Research Grants, 1989*, published annually, Oryx Press, 2214 N. Central at Encato, Phoenix, AZ 85004. $110.

Covers more than 7,000 research grants including those funded by foundations and governmental programs. Known as the *DRG*, this review of funding is one of the best in the research field.

OTHER DIRECTORIES AND AIDS

Some of the other more widely used and helpful resources include:

• *Annual Register of Grant Support: A Directory of Funding Sources: 1990*, 23rd edition. National Register Publishing Company, MacMillan Directory Division, 3004 Glenview Road, Wilmette, IL 60091. 1989. $130.

Over 1,000 pages listing and indexing more than 3,000 funding sources including foundations and government agencies indexed by subject, program, and geography.

• *Handicapped Funding Directory*, 6th edition, Richard M. Eckstein, Research Grant Guides, P.O. Box 4970, Margate, FL 33063. 1989. $29.50.

Profiles of more than 850 foundations and corporations as well as federal sources of support for programs for the disabled.

• *The Grants Register*, St. Martin's Press, 175 Fifth Avenue, New York, NY 10010. Published biennially. $75.

A good listing of grants, scholarships, travel grants, and the like.

• *Preparing Instructional Objectives*, Robert F. Mager, David S. Lake Publishers, 19 Davis Drive, Belmont, CA 94002. $10.95.

A short but classic introduction to how to work objectives in the education field.

Taft Publications
The Taft Group
Suite 450
12300 Twinbrook Parkway
Rockville, MD 20852-9830
(1-800-888-TAFT)

The Taft Group is a commercial company that has been publishing materials in the grants field for many years. Included in its publication list are:

• *America's Newest Foundations: The Sourcebook On Recently Created Philanthropies: 1990*. Descriptions of more than 2,600 new foundations, listed alphabetically by state in the 1990

4th edition including grant type and recipient type indexes. $130.

• *Fund Raiser's Guide to Human Service Funding.* A directory of 900 foundations and corporations that grant funds in the human service field. $110.

• *Taft Foundation Reporter.* Describes all of the largest foundations. Two monthly supplements, *The Foundation Giving Watch* and *Foundation Updates* provide up-to-date information on foundations including changes in funding policies. $397 for the package. $135 for *Giving Watch* only.

• *Taft Corporate Giving Directory.* Complete information on 550 corporate giving programs. Two monthly supplements, *Corporate Giving Watch* and *Corporate Giving Profiles*, provide up-to-date information on new developments and changes. The package can be obtained for $397. For $667 the foundation (listed above) *and* the corporate systems can be ordered together.

Taft also makes available the following books on proposal writing:

• *How to Write Successful Foundation Presentations*, by Joseph Dermer, presents a variety of examples of appeals written to foundations.

• *How to Write Successful Corporate Appeals—With Examples*, by James P. Sinclair, is geared to the special attributes of proposals and letters that go to corporations for funding.

• *The Proposal Writer's Swipe File: 15 Winning Fund-Raising Proposals.* More examples of proposals written by six experienced proposal writers.

• *Grant Proposals That Succeeded*, edited by Virginia White. Examples of successful proposals and explanations of how they were developed. $25.

• *Corporate Philanthropy Report*, published by Craig Smith, 2727 Fairview Avenue East, Seattle, WA 98102

A lively, well-organized newsletter about developments in the corporate giving field and descriptions of giving by companies in different fields such as airlines, communications, and the like. $150 or $128 per year for nonprofits.

• *Government Information Services Publications, 1611 North Kent St., Arlington, VA 22209*

Publishes, in cooperation with the Education Funding Research Council, some nineteen newsletters and special reports on federal, state, and local funding programs and opportunities. Titles include *Local/State Funding Report, Federal Funding Guide, Minority Funding Report, Arts and Culture Funding Report.* Cost for the 50 weekly Local/State reports is, as an example, $297. Puts outs special reports such as *Funding Opportunities in the Drug Law,* $88.95.

• *Health Affairs,* Project HOPE Health Sciences Education Center, Millwood, VA 22646

A newsletter of developments in the health field including "GrantWatch" which covers news of foundations trends and grant announcements in the health field. $55 for institutions, $35 for individuals.

• *Grants for Nonprofit Organizations: A Guide to Funding and Grant Writing,* by Eleanor Gilpatrick, Praeger Books, 88 Post Road West, Box 5007, Westport, CT 06881. $37.95. 1989.

A guide to locating funding sources and case examples.

• *Federal Assistance Monitor,* CD Publications, 8555 16th St. #100, Silver Spring, MD 20910. $219.

Twice-a-month summary of grant opportunities based on the announcments in the Federal Register.

• *Directory of Building and Equipment Grants,* Research Grant Guides, P.O. Box 4970, Margate, FL 33063. 1989. $28.50.

A guide to sources of funds for equipment as well as organizations that contribute equipment.

• *Directory of Financial Aids for Women: 1989–90,* Gail Ann Schlachter, Reference Service Press, 1100 Industrial Road, Suite 9, San Carlos, CA 94070. $42.50.

Describes grant sources to support programs for women as well as sources for scholarships, loans, and internships.

• *The Directory of Financial Aids for Minorities*, Gail Ann Schlachter with Sandra E. Goldstein, Reference Service Press, 1100 Industrial Road, Suite 9, San Carlos, CA 94070. $42.50.

Describes grant sources to support programs for minorities as well as sources for scholarships, loans, and internships.

• *Grant Seekers Guide*, 3rd edition. Editors, Jill R. Shellow and Nancy C. Stella for the National Network of Grantmakers. Moyer Bell Limited, Colonial Hill RFD 1, Mount Kisco, NY 10549. 1989. $24.95.

In addition to describing hundreds of grantmakers this book includes a number of articles on proposal presentation and fund-raising that are of interest to grass roots organizations and those devoted to social justice, for example, "Foundation Funding of Progressive Social Movement."

• *America's Invisible Foundations: A Guide to Smaller But Productive Grant-Making Organizations*, Jerry C. Davis, editor, Foundex America, 611 South College Street, Franklin, KY 42134. 1988. $197.

Describes more than 900 foundations indexed by state and includes examples of grants they provided.

• *Director of Women's Funds 1988*, Women and Foundations/ Corporate Philanthropy, 141 Fifth Avenue, 7-S, New York, NY 10010 $10.

A short (54 pages) listing of funding programs for women.

• *The Individual's Guide to Grants*, Judith Margolin, Plenum Publishing Corporation, 233 Spring Street, New York, NY 10013. 1983. $19.95.

A guide to preparing proposals that seek funding for individual (as contrasted with organizational) projects.

9

KEEPING
A GRANT

MOST GRANTS FROM FOUNDATIONS AND GOVERNMENT FUNDERS ARE for a one-year period. Even if the original proposal was for a longer period, the grants will almost always be made on a year-to-year basis. Since most projects require funding for more than a year, it is critical to plan and implement a program to keep a grant and have it renewed. This chapter outlines the five major elements of a program to ensure that a grant is maintained and renewed. These elements are:

- Adhering to funder requirements
- Maintaining positive relationships with funders, the host agency in which the project is located, and with community agencies, organizations, and leaders
- Implementing an effective program of communications and reporting
- Assuring effective program and financial management
- Preparing a successful reapplication or proposal

ADHERE TO FUNDER REQUIREMENTS

The requirements that funders impose on grantees vary greatly depending upon the type of grant and the particular funding source. For instance, grants and contracts from governmental funders have many more requirements than grants from foundations. And funds provided through contracts have more requirements than funds provided through grants.

Typical governmental requirements include:

- Maintenance of financial and program records for a period of some years, although grantees are allowed to use their own record-keeping systems. Records generally must be made accessible to the government

- Submission of periodic program and financial reports

- Cooperation with government audits

- Adherence to government regulations regarding research involving human subjects

- Obtaining prior approval for changes in program, budget, and, in some cases, personnel

- Compliance with federal regulations regarding civil rights and prohibiting discrimination

These requirements are expressed in various federal government management circulars and compliance agreements, in the RFP or RFA, in the policies of the funding organization, and in the letter or contract that authorizes the grant. Copies of these requirements should be obtained from the funding agency.

Foundation requirements, in contrast to those of government funders, are much less stringent. However, there are requirements that must be observed in the administration of foundation grants. Some of these may come from the foundation itself; others may come from the host agency in which a foundation-funded project is taking place. Host agencies, such as universities, that receive federal money for purposes other than the project, are subject to all of the previously noted federal requirements. And these requirements apply to all activities of the agency regardless of whether the specific activity is funded by a foundation or the government.

Foundations often require at least an annual report of program activities and finances. Even if they don't, it is a good idea to take the initiative and prepare such reports for the foundation. In the case of large-scale foundation projects involving grantees in a number of different communities offering similar programs, the foundation may require the projects to agree to cooperate with outside evaluation agencies. Foundations that become aware of problems in the performance of a grantee may often hold up funds until the problem is resolved. If the problem is one of financial management, the foundation may require an independent audit.

Concentrating on funder requirements is often resisted by project directors whose main interest is in the program they are offering. Experience shows, however, that the perception of the quality of one's program by a funder is often based on how efficiently and effectively a project adheres to funder regulations. This factor is so important in keeping a grant that you should impose some of these kinds of requirements on yourself, even if the funder does not prescribe them.

MAINTAIN POSITIVE RELATIONSHIPS

The second aspect of keeping a grant is to work consciously toward maintaining satisfactory relationships with key people in the funding agency and in the host agency in which the project is located. While one may think of projects, agencies, funders, and others as impersonal entities, in the final analysis relationships are mediated between people. The maintenance of good relationships with funders can be furthered by understanding what kinds of problems may occur and what kinds of strategies can be employed. Remember that, whereas some project directors may view the nature of the relationship with a funder as being adversarial, especially if it is a government funder, the real nature of the relationship is one of interdependence. It is in this context that one should approach the problem of maintaining smooth working relationships. To do this systemically one needs to first identify the areas in which problems, other than those of personality may occur. In general most relationships between projects and funders or host agencies occur in connection with:

Finances and purchasing
Staff
Clientele
Program activities
Public relations
Equipment

In dealing with most funders, it will become apparent after some time that more attention is paid to some of these problem areas than others. Once you have determined if there is such a pattern, then special attention can be paid to avoiding difficulties in that particular area through more careful management, and especially by consulting the funder's staff person prior to making decisions.

At times, however, conflict between projects and funders will occur. In such cases a systematic approach to maintaining relationships begins with an understanding of what strategies are open to you as a director of a grant-funded project. In general there are really only four things you can do:

1. Simply comply with whatever the funder sees as the way to resolve the problem.
2. Try to gain the cooperation of the funder through logical argument and the presentation of information, personal contact, consultation, and showing how the project is promoting the interests of the funder.
3. Bargain and negotiate in order to reach a compromise.
4. Appeal to a higher authority to try and reverse or mediate the problem.

Information, personal contact, and attitude are the key ingredients in maintaining good funder relationships. Compliance with requirements and cooperation are preferred strategies. When more conflictual approaches are necessary, good documentation, a positive attitude, personal contact with higher officials if they are being appealed to, and a willingness to recognize that you can't win them all and that what you are seeking is to keep the grant, are the effective approaches to employ. Do not threaten, do not be provocative, and do not argue over unrelated global issues. And always leave the door open to more discussion.

Many a project has been unable to keep its grant because of problems of relationships within the larger host agency or in the community. Funders, in making a grant, are in effect endorsing and legitimating the project. Their name and reputation become associated with what the project does, and adverse public relations can jeopardize future grants. This is not to say that grant-supported projects should only engage in activities that will be "accepted" by everyone. On the contrary, many grants are intended to bring about change in social, economic, political, and environmental conditions. As such, they will be controversial and the grant-supported activities may conflict with programs, practices, and policies in the community.

What is needed under these circumstances, in order to protect the grant and help obtain future funding, is a positive program of consituency building and public relations. As with compliance with regulations, many project heads see these kinds of activities as secondary to the substantive programmatic or research aspects of the grant. But here again, the evidence is that success in refunding is often directly related to the support (even in the face of opposition) that the project enjoys within the host agency and in the community and field in which it operates.

The major strategies that can be employed here include:

Use the media.   Sending out periodic press releases, appearing on local talk shows, sending public service announcements (PSAs) to radio and television stations, and the like keep the project's name in the public eye.

Prepare a newsletter.   Yes, it is true that many newsletters cross everyone's desk. Nevertheless, a monthly newsletter continues to be an excellent way to maintain a positive image of a project.

Use advisory groups.   Involving community leaders, clientele, staff from other agencies, public officials, and others in committees and groups is a good way to maintain a supportive constituency.

Bring in key individuals.   There are usually certain key people such as local legislators and congresspeople whose support for the project can be very helpful. Meet with them, ask their advice, invite them to visit the project.

Create a climate of openness.   Make it clear that people are welcome to visit at any time. Have an occasional open house. Have coffee and refreshments available. Have a suggestion box displayed in a prominent place.

Finally, if funders include a site visit as part of their monitoring and renewal process, be sure the visit is well planned and that every person involved in the project is well prepared for the visit. Make it a hospitable occasion. Give the visitors handouts to take with them. Do not try to cover anything up.

IMPLEMENT EFFECTIVE REPORTING SYSTEMS

Effective communication with funders can go a long way toward helping you keep a grant. No matter how excellent your project may be performing, nobody else is going to know it unless you tell them. Success is not self-evident: It must be communicated. Because of the pressure to start the project and to meet the project's objectives, it is easy to assign secondary importance to developing a systematic reporting effort aimed at keeping funders, host agencies, and other agencies informed. Among the main kinds of reports that should be included in such an effort are:

- Periodic progress reports on the implementation of the funded work to the funder
- Periodic financial reports to funders
- A final report to the funder on program implementation and finances to the funder
- Periodic reports to the host agency on the progress in implementing the project
- Internal progress reports to the staff of the project itself
- Interpretive reports to community organizations, profes-

sional groups, and key officials and other leaders in the community

Most funders do not have forms to use for reporting progress, but their expectations are similar. They want the reports to be clear, accurate, as brief as possible, and specific to the project.

Here are some guidelines to help maintain a more effective reporting program:

Plan ahead. The most frequent problem in preparing reports is that they are done at the last minute. Prepare a timetable listing each report to be prepared, when to start and finish it, and who is in charge of getting it done.

Make sure the information is available. Design a system to file, manually or by computer, the program and financial information needed for the various reports.

Make your reports distinctive. Decide on a layout for your reports that will make them stand out. Use the same format for every report. Keep the format simple. Don't mix type styles. Use a lot of headings. A heavy bar at the top of every page in every report is an easy way to give your reports their own identity. Or, put the name of the project in small type at the top or bottom of every page.

Use graphics. Use bullets for lists, bar charts, pie charts, and line charts. Place material you want to emphasize in a box (never a circle). Use case examples and references to newspaper and other coverage when it exists.

Check every report. Check for internal consistency and for consistency with prior reports. Credibility of the project can suffer when it becomes apparent to the funder that one progress report or financial report contradicts another.

Follow formats. In those cases where funders have their own stated formats, forms, outlines, or standards for reports, be sure to follow them. Keep a copy of the RFP or RFA since these often prescribe the format, standards, and schedule for submission of program and financial reports.

Finally, an effective reporting system needs to have someone on the project staff designated as the person responsible for the coordination of the program. And someone needs to be designated to check all written material for accuracy and clarity.

EFFECTIVE MANAGEMENT

Funders assume that the projects they support will be effectively and efficiently managed. Keeping a grant depends upon meeting that expectation. Management effectiveness is communicated to funders in their dealings with project directors, through the reports they receive from the project, from things they may hear in the community, and from their own informal or formal observations of the project.

Remember that the perceptions that funders have of the project are just as valid as "what the actual facts are." Therefore, it is helpful to have in mind the areas in which projects tend to run into management difficulties that can jeopardize their grants, either at the present or in the future. The most important factors include:

Leadership style. Project directors need to appear to be in charge and know what they are doing. Periodic contact with the funding agency to report on progress, good written reports, and errorless financial management and reports can contribute to projecting a positive picture of leadership.

Quality of staff. The qualifications of the staff stand as a proxy for measuring program effectiveness. Selecting staff with the best formal qualifications of training and experience as outlined in the original proposal is the way to accomplish this.

Organizational structure. In the case of projects that have a number of different major program activities and large staffs, effective management can be furthered by creating a formal structure in which specific units of the organization have responsibility for specific activities and in which each staff member has clearly assigned responsibilities. Otherwise, the organizational arrangements cannot be understood by those outside the project. And this lack of understanding can lead to negative conclusions regarding the effectiveness of the project's management.

Achieving objectives. Funders provide their money in order to have projects achieve certain specified objectives. A project that can provide evidence that its objectives are or have been achieved is thought to be well managed. One that does not is often seen as poorly managed. Thus, it is wise to use the project's stated objectives as the basis for managing its activities and for measuring the performance of its various units and staff.

Performing on time. One of the problems that can contribute to a negative perception of managerial effectiveness is the failure to complete work within the timetable originally indicated in the proposal. Using the proposal timetable or GANTT chart as a management tool can help to keep a project on schedule.

Responding to crises. Most projects, during the course of the year, face one or more crises—a loss of heat, a loss of staff, a poor story in the local newspaper, criticism from a community leader. Funders are not surprised when these crises occur. What is critically important, however, is how the project responds to such problems. Was it able to make quick arrangements for temporary site? Did it replace a staff person quickly? Did it issue a factual story to rebut criticism? These are the responses that will be looked for in judging the effectiveness of project management.

Financial know-how. Fiscal problems can injure a project's chances for re-funding no matter how good the program may be. Unfortunately, some project heads pay little attention to this aspect of the project's operation or delegate it to another staff person. Four things need to be done in relation to financial management in order to assure keeping a grant. First, there must be a suitable program of financial accounting. This is best set up by an accountant or fiscal expert. Second, there needs to be adequate internal fiscal control exercised by the project head by examining the project's expenditures and income on a regular basis to be sure the project is living within its budget. Third, the project director needs to be thoroughly conversant with the project's budget and with the language and rules that apply to the project's fiscal operations. He or she should be able to communicate this understanding in the course of contacts with the funder. Finally, all financial reports must be properly and accurately submitted to the funder.

PREPARE FOR REFUNDING

It's never too soon to begin planning for the refunding of the project. In some cases the funder may have approved funding for a two- or three-year period and refunding will be subject to submission of an acceptable progress report. In other cases refunding may require submitting a new proposal that focuses on the changes that will occur in the next year in the way of program and financial support. In still other cases an entirely new proposal will be required. In any of these cases some activities should be undertaken to help increase your chances of keeping a grant. These steps include:

1. Building files of material that can be used for refunding purposes from the very minute the project begins

2. Assigning the responsibility for the progress report or new proposal to a staff person well before it is necessary to write and submit the proposal

3. Exploring the various resources to identify additional funding sources to finance a part of the program in the future or to help finance expansions or extension of the program into new areas

4. Orienting all of the staff members to the fact that their day-to-day performance is one of the important factors in assuring continued funding for the project

5. Viewing all aspects of the project, its management, its program, its relationships, its compliance with funder requirements, and all of its reports as having an influence on keeping a grant.

SAMPLE PROGRAM PROPOSAL AND CRITIQUE

This appendix includes a sample program proposal accompanied by a critique pointing out its strengths and weaknesses. For illustrative purposes, a proposal to establish a multiservice center as a decentralized branch of a larger citywide agency has been chosen. This proposal clarifies most of the essential points and is typical of the various issues that must be addressed in many program proposals. The sample proposal omits a budget and timetable since these are illustrated in chapter 4.

PROPOSAL	CRITIQUE

TITLE PAGE

A Proposal to Establish a
Community-Based Multiservice
Center

June 1990

Submitted by
The Plainview
Service Organization
10 Plainview Avenue
Plainview, New York 11000
Telephone (516) 516-5166

INTRODUCTION, PURPOSE, AND OBJECTIVES

This proposal from the Plainview Service Organization (PSO) is to establish a community-based multiservice center offering a variety of alternative mental health services to individuals, families, and the community in the town of Plainview, located in Plainview County, N.Y.

The PSO is a voluntary nonprofit agency that has served Plainview County, whose current population is 1 million, since 1945. Its total operating budget of $2 million comes from

The format for this title page is good. It is descriptive, providing all the essential information. It does not show the amount requested or the funding source to whom it is submitted (optional). This could be done by placing an additional phrase at the bottom that would read:

Submitted to:
The ABC Foundation
10 Avenue L
New York, New York 10080
Request $200,000

The title of the proposal, however, is misleading, since the larger part of the proposal that follows is addressed to establishing services that are alternatives to existing programs. Thus, the title would be more descriptive if the word "Alternative" were added before the word "Multiservice."

A good opening sentence, which covers the name of the applicant, the general contents of the program, and its location.

The proposal attempts to establish PSO's credentials, without going into detail, in the body of the proposal. The detail is presented in a separate capability statement. The reader's at-

PROPOSAL	CRITIQUE

the United Fund and federal and state grants. Originally established as a family counseling and home nursing agency, the PSO, for the last ten years, has changed its focus to concentrate on developing and demonstrating a variety of services aimed at meeting newly identified specialized needs of minorities, aged, and children.* This proposal is in keeping with this focus in that it addresses the emerging needs for preventive and advocacy programs in the field of mental health and particularly for released mental patients.

Through this proposed program a number of urgent needs in Plainview are addressed including (1) the failure of existing agencies, particularly the Welfare Department and mental health clinics, to provide sorely needed prevention-oriented services, (2) the lack of direction of both state and county agencies in the area of mental health in Plainview, (3) the inability of these agencies to serve an advocacy role for minorities and the poor, (4) the frequently inaccessible and fragmenting nature of these programs, and (5) the absence of recognizable communities within Plainview to

tention is directed to the statement by a footnote. Some proposal writers prefer a longer statement about the sponsoring organization at this point in the proposal.

The focus of the proposal on mental health is established early in the introduction. At this point the emphasis on prevention and on released mental patients is established, still very early in the proposal. It is done in a way to entice the reader to go further.

It is appropriate in the Introduction to briefly describe the nature of the problem that is being addressed, as is done here. However, in this proposal the problem is defined largely in terms of the limitations of existing agencies and theory or ideologies (i.e., the definition of mental illness and its causes). The proposal would be strengthened with more specificity in the Introduction, such as the gross number of persons served by mental health agencies, the number released from hospitals, the number requiring prevention, a specific example of "lack of direction" and other needs. Although all this will be dealt with in detail in the Needs section, some concrete needs infor-

*The Capability Statement attached to this proposal details the long and successful experience of the PSO and describes the current resources of the organization.

PROPOSAL	CRITIQUE

actually serve the social needs of residents.

These problems are further aggravated because of a lack of clarity over the definition of mental health and the causes of mental illness. The social implication of mental illness is the fact that individuals who are affected emotionally and psychologically by economic and social situations have been undermined or largely ignored by existing mental health programs.

We would like to state, as our overriding concern and operating principle, that problems in living, presently identified by professionals and the public as psychological, and defined as character defects, many times stem from lack of educational, economic, and social resources, as well as from an underlying inequality between races and sexes. It is also evident to us that if communities provided supportive, comprehensive services aimed at prevention, education, and counseling in areas such as health, law, jobs, and housing, they might be able to curb the spiraling number of people who, as a last resort, are committed to or in desperation commit themselves to mental institutions, because their basic problems in living were not dealt with in their families or in the communities where they live.

There is a pressing need for alternative approaches to com-

mation can be useful in the Introduction to guard against readers being turned off by what they may consider vague ideas.

Phrases such as "economic and social resources" can often be made stronger and more convincing by giving examples. In this case, "for example, housing, transportation, legal aid."

The definition of the *purpose* of this proposal is weak in that (1) it does not go on to say *what* the broad goal is that would be accomplished by "responding to community needs," (2) it does not say directly whether "education and prevention" referred to in the prior sentence will be offered, and (3) it does not indicate whether areas such as "health, law, jobs, and housing," referred to in the previous paragraph, would be covered. The objectives do help to clarify points 1 and 2. There is also a problem in using "education, prevention, and counseling" as

PROPOSAL	CRITIQUE

munity mental health care, which would have as their primary focus education and prevention within the community. The purpose of a multiservice community center would be to offer a well-coordinated, central community base that would respond to a wide, yet specific range of community needs. In addition, it is hoped that such a center would bring together people with common needs and problems, and with the help of staff and coordinated resources, help them to find collective solutions and viable alternatives to their present solutions.

The major objectives of this program are:

(1) To help people achieve a larger measure of self-determination and to create options by providing individual and group counseling regarding legal problems, family problems, family planning, and daycare, health and nutrition, education, jobs, and housing; (2) To provide a central and accessible service for the community; (3) To involve community residents in the planning and implementation of services, thereby assuring a greater degree of community involvement and control; (4) To serve as an information and referral center, and to coordinate data on existing social service agencies in the area; (5) To establish communication with and promote sharing of resources by

if they were separate services, since education can contribute to prevention, as can counseling. Further, there is a need to be specific about what is being prevented. Is it admission or readmission to state hospitals? Is mental disorder being prevented? Some of these questions are clarified later in the proposal, but it is a mistake not to be clear as early as possible. For example, "prevention of mental illness and hospitalization" is mentioned later in objective 6. If this is the main thrust of the proposal, it should be mentioned earlier and added to the statement of purpose. Thus, the purpose would read ". . . range of community needs *in order* to prevent mental illness and hospitalization."

If this is the overall purpose or goal, the *objectives* should state the strategy for achieving this goal in terms of what would be done *and* which results would be *achieved*. As expressed in this proposal, the objectives do indicate what would be done. However, they do not indicate what would be *achieved*. The objectives would be improved by adding to each one some indication of which results would be expected. For example, objective 1 might have added to it, "in order to *reduce* the extent to which these problems negatively affect people's ability to function in the family and community." Or,

PROPOSAL	CRITIQUE
various groups within the community such as civic and church groups; and (6) To evaluate this program as a possible model for effectiveness in the field of community mental health for the prevention of mental illness and hospitalization.	the following could be added, "in order to *increase* people's ability to cope with these problems of daily living." Similar phrases should be added to each objective, thereby making their connection to the prevention of mental illness and hospitalization clearer and more explicit. Doing this also presents the objectives in measurable terms and therefore contributes to the ability to design an evaluation of this program.
	For each objective, one should ask and answer the question "What will be accomplished and will this contribute to achieving the overall purpose or goal?"
	The inclusion of an evaluation objective such as 6 dictates the necessity to have a later section of the proposal on evaluation.

NEED AND RATIONALE

PROPOSAL	CRITIQUE
It was stated in the previous section of this proposal that mental health services in Plainview are failing to meet the public's needs. We would like to examine reasons for this, and to present our rationale for what we believe is a viable alternative to present mental health care.	It helps to convey the coherence and unity of the proposal to show the linkage of one section to another as is done here in the first sentence of the Need section.

PROPOSAL	CRITIQUE

NEED

It is ironic that a county that houses more than one-third (approximately 19,000) of the state's mental patients is one of the most backward in the nation in terms of offering innovative and preventive mental health services. At present count, Plainview has only four county-run mental health clinics, and fewer than a dozen private-contract (contracted by the county) agencies to service a population of 1 million in an area of over 500 square miles. There is only one crisis-telephone hotline, and no half-way houses in the county.

This statement would be strengthened by indicating the number served by the "four county-run clinics" and relating this number to an overall indicator of need. This would help convince the reader of the inadequacy of present services.

Although there are no formal data available on the effectiveness of services or treatment offered in these mental health clinics, it is obvious to the participant or observer that they are grossly understaffed, that waiting lists are long, that they cater primarily to white clients with incomes well above the poverty level, and that they are staffed with white professionals (as well as a large number of foreign-born psychiatrists who have difficulty communicating with clients).

The word "data" is always plural; thus, it should be used with the verb "are" not the verb "is."

This criticism would be more convincing if the writer had taken the time to obtain some figures on number of staff and number and characteristics of clients from available agency reports. Using such figures also helps establish the credibility of the proposal sponsors.

It is also apparent that these clinics are still relying on outdated and—particularly for low-income and minority people—irrelevant modes of intervention and treatment. They are staffed

Again, some form of documentation would strengthen the argument in this paragraph. Documentation is needed to make it more persuasive and encourage the reader to have confidence in its validity.

PROPOSAL	CRITIQUE
with traditionally trained psychiatrists, psychologists, and social workers, whose practice is limited generally to individual, family, and group insight therapy. Piecemeal attempts are made to assist people with problems other than psychiatric, i.e., job, school, financial, and legal problems, to name a few. There is little coordination with other service agencies such as welfare, legal aid, or public health clinics. The basic orientation is toward remedial crisis, rather than preventive programs designed to alleviate the cause preceding and underlying the crisis.	This is a good example of internal consistency; the proposal links the need with the purpose (i.e., prevention).
It has been our experience that people apply to these clinics in desperation and as a last resort, when problems have snowballed and assumed crisis proportions. In line with this, there is little if any outreach to the surrounding community or catchment area that the clinic supposedly serves.	
Why such glaring inadequacies in the service system? We see one reason having to do with the conflict of interest between state and county over control and financing of mental health services. Another reason is that the helping professions' operating principle is based on the medical model,* in which peo-	It is important always to define specialized terminology such as "medical model," as is done in the footnote.

*The medical model views mental disturbance as disease oriented and rooted in individual pathology.

PROPOSAL	CRITIQUE
ple's problems are seen as purely psychological in origin and in manifestation. The psychiatric profession has always been resistant to seeing mental illness in any other terms than psychological. The sad fact is that social services, and particularly mental health services, are oriented to keeping the profession constant and stable rather than to meet the needs of the people being served.	To use global generalities, as done here, regarding psychiatric and mental health services can discredit the proposal. Better wording might be "many members of the psychiatric profession have been resistant . . ."
In line with our observations of the inadequacies of services, we think the following summaries of research findings amply demonstrate the need for a qualitatively different approach in the design and delivery of mental health services:	
1. The roots of mental illness are in the social environment, not in the individual (Hollingshead and Redlich, Srole, Langner and Michael, Peck, Kaplan and Roman).	This is a good demonstration of building the proposal's credibility, since it shows that the writers know the mental health field. However, footnotes or a bibliography should accompany the text, giving the full references.
2. The lower the socioeconomic class, the higher the rate of mental illness (Hollingshead, report of Joint Commission of Mental Health).	
3. Poverty and racism are in large part responsible for major mental health problems (Joint Commission on Mental Health).	Notice also that the writers in presenting this material have gotten away from the global black-or-white generalities that characterize the earlier part of this section of the proposal.
4. Poor people are much more reluctant to seek help from psychiatric clinics (Avnet, Hollingshead).	
5. Mental health clinic staff	

PROPOSAL	CRITIQUE

tend to treat their own kind (white, middle class) (Adams and McDonald, Broverman).

6. Mental hospitalization greatly increases during economic downturns and decreases during upturns (Brenner).

What these research findings indicate is not a justification for expansion of the existing service system, but an entire restructuring of it. Since mental health is directly related to one's educational, economic, and social situation, we must take a multidimensional approach to help remedy the multitude of related social factors that cause people to become "mentally ill." The one-dimensional, clinically oriented approach that views people as enclosed psychiatric entities is not a sufficient answer.

RATIONALE

In proposing a multiservice community center, we aim to provide a form of service that is primarily dictated by the particular conditions prevailing in the community. Any form of intervention undertaken must consider these conditions (and their effects on the individual) before effective service can be provided. What is needed is a basic orientation to social action and, ultimately, change, deempha-

Whenever research or other work is cited, it is good proposal writing to indicate the implications and relevance of these references to the program being proposed. This is skillfully handled in this paragraph.

The Need section is well done but would be more convincing with additional concrete documentation of the nature and extent of the problem.

In this sample proposal the Rationale is incorporated with the statement of Need. It could also be a separate section or the first part of the Program section. Regardless of format, the content of the rationale should set the stage for the program description and should also serve to justify the proposed program activities.

PROPOSAL	CRITIQUE

sizing traditional clinical goals of adjustment to what is.

Three measures that we view as necessary vehicles for change are prevention, advocacy, and education. In order to realize our goals we will (1) need professionals and community people alike who are willing to act as advocates for clients first, before the needs of any particular institution or agency. We will seek out and attempt to work closely with other agencies dedicated to advocacy, such as People for Adequate Service and the Local Action Committee. (2) We need to work toward prevention of overwhelming stress situations that all too frequently result in mental hospitalization. To do this, we need to provide encouragement and direct assistance in formulating specific needs, stating complaints, and asserting basic rights. (3) We need to educate people regarding their basic rights: to receive adequate public assistance, their legal options and rights, decent housing, free or low-cost quality care for children, medical care, consumer rights. (4) We need to provide a focal point within the community for residents to work together on, and receive assistance with, their basic problems in living.

We chose the community of Plainview for our pilot project because it presents the greatest need in terms of relevant social

When reference to cooperating agencies is made, there should be some description of them and supporting letters from these agencies.

Notice that the rationale is stressing *advocacy*. From the standpoint of internal consistency, the proposal writers should have highlighted the advocacy approach in the Introduction and Need sections. The writers need to go back and consider revising the Introduction and the statements of purpose and objectives to be sure that they are consistent with the advocacy approach that is developed in this section.

PROPOSAL	CRITIQUE
services. In comparison with the rest of the county, it has one of the highest unemployment rates and number of people receiving public assistance; one of the lowest in terms of median income and educational attainment. In addition, there is evidence of a lack of decent and sufficient housing as well as wide-scale housing discrimination. Although conclusive figures are not available, it is estimated that admission rates to state hospitals are significantly higher from this area.	The writers have introduced needs material as part of the Rationale. This may be appropriate if the detailed statements documenting the high unemployment, public assistance, and other rates referred to are already presented in the Need section. In this proposal they were not included. The writers need to go back and add this material to the Need section.
We recognize that an attempt to change the present service system, and to reorder priorities of mental health care, will not happen overnight. One community center will certainly not cure the ills of an entire system. We are well aware of the fact that unless the poor have some gain in their economic situation, self-sufficiency and determination will not be attained; of fundamental importance is basic income support for poor people.	This is an example of how to recognize the limitations of the proposal in a way that contributes to the proposal's credibility.
Yet we must, at some point, begin to address people's priorities. Evidence strongly supports organizing and offering alternatives at the community level. With a maximum amount of planning and participation by residents, a sizable contribution can be made to the mental health and well-being of the community as a whole.	The limitations are not just left standing. The writers attempt to show that in spite of the limitations the proposed program is a valuable undertaking, which will result in benefits to the community. They could have gone on to explain how, through the evaluation, the program would also contribute to developing new approaches that

PROPOSAL	CRITIQUE

PROGRAM DESIGN

To accomplish the objectives set forth in this proposal, the following coordination and program design will be implemented.

PROGRAM DEVELOPMENT AND COORDINATION

The first step in the coordination of the Multiservice Community Center will be the formation of a *Community Advisory Committee*. Membership will include the PSO's board of directors, leaders of civic, church, and community groups, and consumer representatives drawn from the community at large. The committee will be responsible initially for (1) location of a suitable site for the Center; (2) promotion and publicity of the program by way of intensive mass-media publicity, and outreach to community residents and organizations; (3) establishment of program policies; (4) election of a board of directors; and (5) recommendations for hiring of staff.

TRAINING AND RECRUITMENT OF STAFF

Staff will be recruited on the basis of experience, knowledge of,

---

can be adopted in other places.

The writers again show the linkage between the objectives and the specific program activities.

Instead of stressing the area of "coordination," it would be more to the point to talk about planning and development of the "Center." It makes a proposal much clearer to list each specific program activity with separate headings, as the writers have done in this entire section. However, in doing so it is important that the headings be clear. Further, the headings in the program section should be as active as possible, so that they denote specific tasks to be done. The initial part of this section of the proposal could have been organized more effectively if there were one general heading such as "1. Program Development" and then subheadings such as:

A. Appointment of Advisory Committee
B. Recruitment and Training of Staff
C. Location of Site

PROPOSAL	CRITIQUE

and familiarity with, the basic objectives of the Center program. Staff will be recruited, to the extent possible, from the Plainview area through newspaper advertising, notices in prominent locations throughout the area, and recommendations from the advisory committee. Final selection of staff will be determined by the board of directors of PSO.

An initial training program will be instituted for new staff, and in addition, an ongoing training program will be provided for Center staff and interested community residents. The training will be directed at developing indigenous leadership and expertise within the community, both at the professional and communal levels.

PROGRAM ACTIVITIES

The Center will be located in a central section of Plainview, readily accessible to railway and local bus service. It will be open six days a week, Monday through Saturday. Services will be available during both day and evening hours, and transportation will be provided to and from the Center when necessary.

Open forums will be held regularly at the Center on issues of particular interest to staff and community, such as the housing dilemma, welfare rights, employment, etc. These forums

D. Establishment of Program Policies
E. Publicizing the Program

Under each of these headings there should be a narrative of the tasks that would go into the activity and the way in which these tasks would be carried out.

Since in describing these program activities it is necessary to refer to certain aspects of the overall administrative structure, it is good practice to also refer the reader to the section of the proposal where the administrative structure is described in more detail.

The program activities or services of the Center are well grouped in this part of the proposal. Their presentation would be enhanced if the writers were more direct in showing the relationship of these activities to the objectives. This can be done in two ways. First by showing which activities are related to which objectives. The writers have done some of this under Structured Group Workshops, in their discussion of the purpose of the workshops. However, the three purposes listed do not correspond to the way the objectives were stated in the Introduction section of the proposal.

The second way to make the connection between program activities and objectives is to explain how the activity will

PROPOSAL

will be open to the community and representatives from both public and grass-roots organizations will be invited to participate.

Direct Services. *Structured Group Workshops:* The purpose of these workshops is threefold: (1) to educate residents of their rights as citizens; (2) to provide support and encouragement, by both group members and leaders, in exploring alternative solutions to specific problems in living; (3) to assist group members in achieving—collectively—a large measure of self-sufficiency and determination.

The workshops will be run by a professionally trained staff member, experienced in that particular area, in conjunction with one community worker who has, ideally, had experience in negotiating the particular "system" in question (courts, welfare, hospitals).

Both community worker and professional will serve as advocates for group members in naming and following out a course of action. The workshops will be small in size, numbering between six and twelve members, and will meet weekly. Workshops will be organized around the following topic areas, with the understanding that groups will be modified or expanded in accordance with the needs of residents.

CRITIQUE

contribute to accomplishing the objective. The writers have accomplished this in a number of places in their discussion of the workshop activities.

Note that the word "system" so often used in the human service field has been clarified by the writers in the text by giving examples "(courts, welfare, hospitals)."

Although the series of workshops is adequately described in this proposal, the writers have not adequately described how people would be recruited, selected, and admitted into the workshops. This omission is frequent in human service program proposals. It should be handled in a separate subsection on "recruitment and selection of participants" or "intake" or "admission to the program."

The proposal also reveals another weakness that often appears in the program section of human service proposals. That is, it does not provide summaries of the estimated number of people who will be served by each activity and in the aggregate. It also has not adequately described the characteristics of those who would be served in terms of the expected racial, sex, age, and problem backgrounds of the participants. Brief estimates of these items strengthen a proposal, since they convey careful planning and understanding of the program to the funder.

PROPOSAL	CRITIQUE

Legal Assistance Workshop: Will be run by a lawyer employed by the Center whose purpose will be to inform people of the law and their legal rights. The community worker serving as coleader will accompany people to court and legal aid, and in general, act as an advocate for that group member.

Employment Workshop: Will provide counseling regarding (1) careers: helping people decide what field to enter; (2) reentry: helping older people, or those who have been out of work for a long period, to get back into the labor force; (3) job rights: teaching people what their employment rights are under the law; how to fight job discrimination when it occurs; procedures for unionizing; where to get specific job training.

Education Workshop: To assist those interested in further education to (1) identify and evaluate the skills they already have developed—either through life experience or jobs; (2) to explore available schools and educational programs and help choose those that best meet the person's needs.

Welfare/Public Assistance Workshop: To educate in regard to welfare rights; to inform of eligibility requirements and regulations of DSS, SSI, Medicaid, and social security; to directly assist in negotiating and receiving these services.

PROPOSAL	CRITIQUE
Health and Nutrition: To be run by a registered nurse employed by the Center and a community worker. Purpose will be to discuss basic health needs and preventive measures, correct diet, and nutrition; and to identify what conditions warrant medical attention. When necessary, direct referrals will be made to the Plainview West Health Center and to the Plainview East Community Health Center.	Note an inconsistency in the titling of these activities. Each of the prior activities included the word "workshop" in the heading. The writers, perhaps in order not to be repetitive, have dropped that word. This inconsistency can raise a question for the reader of whether we are still talking about workshops.
Housing: Purpose will be (1) to directly assist people in securing safe, comfortable, and low-cost housing; (2) to inform people of their rights as tenants; (3) to assist people when faced with housing discrimination; (4) to work in conjunction with other agencies such as Council of Churches Housing Bureau and the local action committee on issues and problems pertaining to housing.	
Family Problems: This group(s) will focus on specific marital problems such as separation and divorce, and examine issues relating to sex roles, the single parent, family planning, and daycare.	
In addition to these workshops, there will be crisis intervention, through both group and individual counseling. The primary purpose of this service will be (1) to offer support to persons who are suicidal and/or who are undergoing enormous stress due	The writers are now describing a different type of program activity—"crisis intervention"—which is not a workshop. A new subheading should be used to emphasize that this is another activity.

PROPOSAL	CRITIQUE

to death of a loved one, overuse of drugs or alcohol, loss of job, failure in school or work, serious physical illness, etc.; (2) to help find an immediate short-term solution to the presenting problem, and (3) to prevent, whenever possible, hospitalization.

A child-care service, run by two community aides, will be provided for residents attending the Center. Referrals will be made to Plainview Head Start and Daycare Center for those needing extended daycare services.

Here is an example of another activity buried in the text. It should be highlighted by using the subheading "Child-Care Services."

Referral Services. The Center will organize and maintain an extensive *Data Bank* for referral services and information concerning jobs, housing, legal services, transportation, schools, consumer information, etc. The entire staff will be responsible for the maintenance and updating of the information and services contained in the bank. Residents referred to other community or service agencies will be urged to give the staff feedback (by way of phone call or short questionnaire) on the agency's responsiveness (or lack of it) to the resident.

Screening of services named in the bank will be an ongoing staff activity. In the initial stages of the program, a representative of the staff will be delegated to visit each agency in the area to determine the nature of and as-

PROPOSAL	CRITIQUE

sess the effectiveness of that agency or program.

COORDINATION WITH OTHER AGENCIES

One of the stated objectives of the program is to promote the sharing of resources and to avoid unnecessary duplication of services. In addition to the regularly held forums, one or two representatives from other agencies within the area will be invited each month to open "community meetings," held at the Center. Initially, these meetings will serve to inform other agencies of our services and activities. The overall, and continuing, purpose of these meetings will be to discuss ways in which collectively we can be more responsive to the needs of the community. Open invitations will be extended to local civic groups and church groups in addition to service agencies.

Here, the writers have successfully made explicit the linkage between a program activity and an objective.

This shows the reader that the proposal writers have a knowledge of how to implement this activity. Giving an indication of the number of groups in the community that would be invited would make this even more convincing.

PROGRAM EVALUATION

As the Multiservice Community Center is to serve as a model program for other communities, a major aspect of its design will be program evaluation. A detailed research design

It is evident that there is not a design for evaluation of the program. The writers are, in effect, saying that they recognize a need for an evaluation but would like to design it later.

PROPOSAL	CRITIQUE
will be developed and implemented in cooperation with the funding agency in the beginning stages of the program. Progress reports will be made regularly.	This may be acceptable to some funders, but it is advisable to clear this with the funding agency before submitting the complete proposal. Many funders would expect a more detailed statement of the evaluation.
Briefly stated here, the evaluation will take into account (1) Utilization of Center services: who attends the Center, how often, under what circumstances; (2) Assessment of residents' attitudes toward and opinions of services; (3) Success in meeting primary goals and objectives; (4) Number of admissions to state hospitals from the Plainview area before and after establishment of the Center; (5) Measurable change within the community; (6) Impact of program on other community agencies.	

ADMINISTRATION AND STAFFING

COMMUNITY ADVISORY COMMITTEE

The Community Advisory Committee will be made up of individuals selected from the PSO Board of Directors, civic, church, and community leaders from within the Plainview community, and community representatives. The Community Advisory Committee will be responsible for making sugges-	The composition and responsibilities of all committees and boards are pointed out in this proposal but it would also be helpful to indicate the number of people who would be on the committee; and, if possible, to list their names and positions.

PROPOSAL	CRITIQUE

tions and recommendations to the Center Board of Directors on matters of program development and services and act as a liaison between the community and Center to assure increased sensitivity toward the community it serves.

BOARD OF DIRECTORS

The existing PSO Board of Directors will act as the primary policy and decision-making body to reflect the needs and scope of the Center as seen by the Community Advisory Committee. The board will meet once a month, and membership will encompass a wide range of business, mental health, legal, and community (both professional and civic) representation from the county.

    The board will be directly responsible for insuring that the Center is continually providing high-quality services; that responsible personnel are staffing the Center and directing their energies to programs that the community wants. The board of directors is the overseer and coordinator of the Center *for the community*. The executive director of the Center will report directly to the board on a monthly basis. The board of directors is also responsible for the maintenance of sound fiscal and personnel policies. Areas involving general responsibilities of

A list of this existing board could be included in the capability statement that will accompany this proposal.

PROPOSAL	CRITIQUE

the Center, especially on internal bases such as personnel and financial matters, will be handled by committees that will report directly to the board.

EXECUTIVE DIRECTOR

The Center director will be responsible for the overall running and day-to-day activities of the program. (S)he will have the major responsibility for the content, direction, and implementation of Center services, as put forth by the board of directors.

    The director will sit on committees set up to coordinate finance, public relations, and personnel, and will report monthly to the board of directors. In addition, the director will work in conjunction with, and delegate responsibility to, two staff coordinators, for the supervision and training of staff.

Qualifications. The position will call for training and experience in the clinical, planning, and community organization aspects of social service delivery.

An organizational chart similar to the example shown in Figure 3 would help to clarify the board, committee, and staff structure that is being proposed.

For positions of major responsibility such as executive directors, a more specific statement of qualifications should be included, explaining minimum education and experience that will be accepted. Such as: "advanced degree in social welfare" and "3–5 years experience in administration of social agencies."

STAFF COORDINATORS

Two full-time positions. Responsible for working in a supervisory

PROPOSAL	CRITIQUE

and training capacity in conjunction with the executive director; in charge of organizing and overseeing the direct-service workshops, referral service, and coordination with other agencies. Will also participate in leading the education, housing, employment, and welfare workshops.

Qualifications. MSW, and minimum of five years' experience in community mental health services; thorough knowledge of the social service agency network.

The writers have, for the positions, provided the specificity they failed to include for other positions.

PSYCHIATRIST

One part-time position. Responsible for heading crisis intervention workshop and individual counseling; making psychiatric evaluations and prescribing and dispensing drugs when necessary. In addition, will participate in training of staff.

Where part-time positions are indicated, the amount of time should be explained, for example, "one half-time" or "100 days."

Qualifications. Position will call for experience with community mental health delivery, both community-clinic and hospital aspects.

PSYCHOLOGIST

One full-time position: will be responsible for running family workshop and share responsibility with the psychiatrist for evaluation and crisis-intervention counseling.

PROPOSAL	CRITIQUE

Qualifications. Training and experience in family counseling and child psychology.

LAWYER

One part-time position; responsible for running legal workshop and consulting with staff on all legal matters.

Qualifications. Legal experience with economic problems, family problems, landlord–tenant problems, and criminal matters. Candidate with job experience in community legal services agency preferred.

NURSE

One full-time RN to run health and nutrition workshop, make referrals to appropriate agencies, such as health clinics and hospitals, and provide individual counseling on matters of health and nutrition.

Qualifications. Extensive experience in public health nursing.

COMMUNITY WORKERS

Two full-time positions for local residents. Responsibilities will include: acting as coleaders for direct service workshops; serving as liaison between clients and staff; acting as advocates for clients; making referrals for cli-

PROPOSAL	CRITIQUE

ents to other agencies when necessary; participating in outreach efforts to inform residents of the programs being offered.

CHILD-CARE WORKERS

Two part-time positions for community residents. Duties will include the supervision and care of children of clients attending the Center.

BUS DRIVER

One full-time position; responsible for transporting residents to and from the Center and, when necessary, to other agencies.

SECRETARY

Two full-time positions. Duties will include: obtaining intake information on new clients; referring clients to appropriate services or staff within the Center; maintaining files, data bank, and correspondence; taking minutes at Center meetings.

In proposals with a fairly large staff complement, it helps to clarify the staffing pattern to include a summary chart that shows each job title, the number of people, and the level of effort (i.e., amount of time). An example of such a summary chart for this proposal is shown in Table 1.

RECEPTIONIST

One full-time position. Responsibilities will be to cover the telephones and to schedule appointments for clients.

Table 1. Summary of Staffing Pattern

POSITION	NUMBER OF PEOPLE	LEVEL OF EFFORT
Executive Director	1	full time
Staff Coordinator	2	full time
Psychiatrist	1	half time
Psychologist	1	full time
Lawyer	1	half time
Nurse	1	full time
Community Workers	2	full time
Child-Care Workers	2	half time
Bus Driver	1	full time
Secretary	2	full time
Receptionist	1	full time

APPENDIX B

THE FOUNDATION CENTER COOPERATING COLLECTIONS NETWORK

FREE FUNDING INFORMATION CENTERS

The Foundation Center is an independent national service organization established by foundations to provide an authoritative source of information on private philanthropic giving. The New York, Washington, DC, Cleveland, and San Francisco reference collections operated by the Foundation Center offer a wide variety of services and comprehensive collections of information on foundations and grants. Cooperating Collections are libraries, community foundations, and other nonprofit agencies that provide a core collection of Foundation Center publications and a variety of supplementary materials and services in areas useful to grantseekers. The core collection consists of:

Foundation Directory
Foundation Fundamentals
Foundation Grants Index

National Directory of Corporate Giving Source Book Profiles

Foundation Grants to Individuals
Literature of the Nonprofit Sector
National Data Book of Foundations

Many of the network members have sets of private foundation information returns (IRS 990-PF) for their state or region which are available for public use. A complete set of U.S. foundation returns can be found at the New York and Washington, DC, offices of the Foundation Center. The Cleveland and San Francisco offices contain IRS 990-PF returns for the midwestern and western states, respectively. Those Cooperating Collections marked with a bullet (•) have sets of private foundation information returns for their state or region.

Because the collections vary in their hours, materials, and services, *it is recommended that you call each collection in advance.* To check on new locations or more current information, call 1–800–424–9836.

REFERENCE COLLECTIONS OPERATED BY THE FOUNDATION CENTER

The Foundation Center
8th Floor
79 Fifth Avenue
New York, NY 10003
212–620–4230

The Foundation Center
Room 312
312 Sutter Street
San Francisco, CA 94108
415–397–0902

The Foundation Center
1001 Connecticut Avenue, NW
Washington, DC 20036
202–331–1400

The Foundation Center
Kent H. Smith Library
1442 Hanna Building
Cleveland, OH 44115
216–861–1933

Alabama
• Birmingham Public Library
  Government Documents
  2100 Park Place
  Birmingham 35203
  205–226–3600

  Huntsville Public Library
  915 Monroe St.
  Huntsville 35801
  205–532–5940

  University of South Alabama
  Library Reference Dept.
  Mobile 36688
  205–460–7025

• Auburn University at Montgomery Library
  1–85 @ Taylor Rd.
  Montgomery 36193–0401
  205–271–9649

Alaska
  University of Alaska
  Anchorage Library
  3211 Providence Drive
  Anchorage 99508
  907–786–1848

Juneau Public Library
292 Marine Way
Juneau 99801
907–586–5249

Arizona
- Phoenix Public Library
  Business & Sciences Dept.
  12 East McDowell Road
  Phoenix 85257
  602–262–4636

- Tuscon Public Library
  200 South Sixth Avenue
  Tucson 85726–7470
  602–791–4393

Arkansas
- Westark Community College Library
  5210 Grand Avenue
  Fort Smith 72913
  501–785–7000

- Central Arkansas Library System
  Reference Services
  700 Louisiana Street
  Little Rock 72201
  501–370–5950

California
- Peninsula Community Foundation
  1204 Burlingame Avenue
  Burlingame 94011–0627
  415–342–2505

- Orange County Community Developmental Council
  1695 W. MacArthur Blvd.
  Costa Mesa 92626
  714–540–9293

- California Community Foundation
  Funding Information Center
  3580 Wilshire Blvd., Suite 1660
  Los Angeles 90010
  213–413–4042

- Community Foundation for Monterey County
  420 Pacific Street
  Monterey 93942
  408–375–9712

Riverside Public Library
3581 7th Street
Riverside 92501
714–782–5201

California State Library
Reference Services, Rm. 301
914 Capitol Mall
Sacramento 95814
916–322–4570

- San Diego Community Foundation
  525 "B" Street, Suite 410
  San Diego 92101
  619–239–8815

- Nonprofit Development
  1762 Technology Dr., Suite 225
  San Jose 95110
  408–452–8181

California Community Foundation
Volunteer Center of Orange County
1000 E. Santa Ana Blvd.
Santa Ana, CA 92701
714–953–1655

- Santa Barbara Public Library
  40 East Anapamu
  Santa Barbara 93101–1603
  805–962–7653

Santa Monica Public Library
1343 Sixth Street
Santa Monica 90401–1603
213–458–8859

Colorado
Pikes Peak Library District
20 North Cascade Avenue
Colorado Springs 80901
719–473–2080

- Denver Public Library
Sociology Division
1357 Broadway
Denver 80203
303–571–2190

Connecticut
Danbury Public Library
170 Main Street
Danbury 06810
203–797–4527

- Hartford Public Library
Reference Department
500 Main Street
Hartford 06103
203–293–6000

D.A.T.A.
25 Science Park
Suite 502
New Haven 06511
203–786–5225

Delaware
- University of Delaware
Hugh Morris Library
Newark 19717–5267
302–451–2965

Florida
Volusia County Library Center
City Island
Daytona Beach 32014–4484
904–255–3765

Nova University
Einstein Library—Foundation Resource Collection
3301 College Avenue
Fort Lauderdale 33314
305–475–7497

Indian River Community College
Learning Resources Center
3209 Virginia Avenue
Fort Pierce 34981–5599
407–468–4757

- Jacksonville Public Libraries
Business, Science & Documents
122 North Ocean Street
Jacksonville 32206
904–630–2665

- Miami-Dade Public Library
Humanities Department
101 W. Flagler St.
Miami 33130
305–375–2665

- Orlando Public Library
Orange County Library System
101 E. Central Blvd.
Orlando 32801
407–425–4694

Selby Public Library
1001 Boulevard of the Arts
Sarasota 34236
813–951–5501

- Leon County Public Library
Funding Resource Center
1940 North Monroe Street
Tallahassee 32303
904–487–2665

Palm Beach County Community
Foundation
324 Datura Street, Suite 340
West Palm Beach 33401
407–659–6800

Georgia
- Atlanta-Fulton Public Library
Foundation Collection—Ivan Allen Department
1 Margaret Mitchell Square
Atlanta 30303–1089
404–730–1900

Hawaii
- Hawaii Community Foundation
  Hawaii Resource Room
  212 Merchant Street
  Suite 330
  Honolulu 96813
  808–599–5767

  University of Hawaii
  Thomas Hale Hamilton Library
  2550 The Mall
  Honolulu 96822
  808–948–7214

Idaho
- Boise Public Library
  715 S. Capitol Blvd.
  Boise 83702
  208–384–4024

- Caldwell Public Library
  1010 Dearborn Street
  Caldwell 83605
  208–459–3242

Illinois
  Belleville Public Library
  121 East Washington Street
  Belleville 62220
  618–234–0441

- Donors Forum of Chicago
  53 W. Jackson Blvd., Rm. 430
  Chicago 60604
  312–431–0265

- Evanston Public Library
  1703 Orrington Avenue
  Evanston 60201
  312–866–0305

- Sangamon State University Library
  Shepherd Road
  Springfield 62794–9243
  217–786–6633

Indiana
- Allen County Public Library
  900 Webster Street
  Fort Wayne 46802
  219–424–7241

  Indiana University Northwest Library
  3400 Broadway
  Gary 46408
  219–980–6582

- Indianapolis–Marion County
  Public Library
  40 East St. Clair Street
  Indianapolis 46206
  317–269–1733

Iowa
- Cedar Rapids Public Library
  Funding Information Center
  500 First Street, SE
  Cedar Rapids 52401
  319–398–5145

  Southwestern Community College
  Learning Resource Center
  1501 W. Townline Rd.
  Creston 50801
  515–782–7081, ext. 262

- Public Library of Des Moines
  100 Locust Street
  Des Moines 50308
  515–283–4152

Kansas
- Topeka Public Library
  1515 West Tenth Street
  Topeka 66604
  913–233–2040

- Wichita Public Library
  223 South Main
  Wichita 67202
  316–262–0611

Kentucky

Western Kentucky University
Helm-Cravens Library
Bowling Green 42101
502–745–6122

- Louisville Free Public Library
  Fourth and York Streets
  Louisville 40203
  502–561–8617

Louisiana

- East Baton Rouge Parish Library
  Centroplex Branch
  120 St. Louis Street
  Baton Rouge 70802
  504–389–4960

- New Orleans Public Library
  Business and Science Division
  219 Loyola Avenue
  New Orleans 70140
  504–596–2580

- Shreve Memorial Library
  424 Texas Street
  Shreveport 71120–1523
  318–226–5894

Maine

- University of Southern Maine
  Office of Sponsored Research
  246 Deering Ave., Rm. 628
  Portland 04103
  207–780–4871

Maryland

- Enoch Pratt Free Library
  Social Science and History Department
  400 Cathedral Street
  Baltimore 21201
  301–396–5320

Massachusetts

- Associated Grantmakers of Massachusetts
  294 Washington Street
  Suite 840
  Boston 02108
  617–426–2608

- Boston Public Library
  666 Boylston St.
  Boston 02117
  617–536–5400

- Western Massachusetts Funding Resource Center
  Campaign for Human Development
  73 Chestnut Street
  Springfield 01103
  413–732–3175

- Worcester Public Library
  Grants Resource Center
  Salem Square
  Worcester 01608
  508–799–1655

Michigan

- Alpena County Library
  211 North First Avenue
  Alpena 49707
  517–356–6188

  University of Michigan–Ann Arbor
  209 Hatcher Graduate Library
  Ann Arbor 48109–1205
  313–764–1149

- Henry Ford Centennial Library
  16301 Michigan Avenue
  Dearborn 48126
  313–943–2330

- Wayne State University
  Purdy-Kresge Library
  5265 Cass Avenue
  Detroit 48202
  313–577–6424

- Michigan State University Libraries
  Reference Library
  East Lansing 48824–1048
  517–353–8818

- Farmington Community Library
  32737 West 12 Mile Road
  Farmington Hills 48018
  313–553–0300

- University of Michigan–Flint Library
  Reference Department
  Flint 48502–2186
  313–762–3408

- Grand Rapids Public Library
  Business Dept.
  60 Library Plaza NE
  Grand Rapids 49503–3093
  616–456–3600

- Michigan Technological University Library
  Highway U.S. 41
  Houghton 49931
  906–487–2507

- Sault Ste. Marie Area Public Schools
  Office of Compensatory Education
  460 W. Spruce St.
  Sault Ste. Marie 49783–1874
  906–635–6619

Minnesota
- Duluth Public Library
  520 W. Superior Street
  Duluth 55802
  218–723–3802

  Southwest State University Library
  Marshall 56258
  507–537–7278

Minneapolis Public Library
Sociology Department
300 Nicollet Mall
Minneapolis 55401
612–372–6555

Rochester Public Library
11 First Street, SE
Rochester 55902–3743
507–285–8002

St. Paul Public Library
90 West Fourth Street
Saint Paul 55102
612–292–6307

Mississippi
Jackson/Hinds Library System
300 North State Street
Jackson 39201
601–968–5803

Missouri
- Clearinghouse for Midcontinent Foundations
  Univ. of Missouri
  Law School, Suite 1-300
  52nd Street and Oak
  Kansas City 64113–0680
  816–276–1176

- Kansas City Public Library
  311 East 12th Street
  Kansas City 64106
  816–221–9650

- Metropolitan Association for Philanthropy, Inc.
  5585 Pershing Avenue
  Suite 150
  St. Louis 63112
  314–361–3900

- Springfield–Greene County Library
  397 East Central Street
  Springfield 65801
  417–866–4636

Montana
- Eastern Montana College Library
  1500 N. 30th Street
  Billings 59101–0298
  406–657–1662

- Montana State Library
  Reference Department
  1515 E. 6th Avenue
  Helena 59620
  406–444–3004

Nebraska
- University of Nebraska
  106 Love Library
  14th & R Streets
  Lincoln 68588–0410
  402–472–2848

- W. Dale Clark Library
  Social Sciences Department
  215 South 15th Street
  Omaha 68102
  402–444–4826

Nevada
- Las Vegas–Clark County Library
  District
  1401 East Flamingo Road
  Las Vegas 89119–6160
  702–733–7810

- Washoe County Library
  301 South Center Street
  Reno 89501
  702–785–4012

New Hampshire
- New Hampshire Charitable Fund
  One South Street
  Concord 03302–1335
  603–225–6641

New Jersey
  Cumberland County Library
  800 E. Commerce Street
  Bridgeton 08302–2295
  609–453–2210

The Support Center
17 Academy Street, Suite 1101
Newark 07102
201–643–5774

County College of Morris
Masten Learning Resource Center
Route 10 and Center Grove Rd.
Randolph 07869
201–361–5000 ext. 470

- New Jersey State Library
  Governmental Reference
  185 West State Street
  Trenton 08625–0520
  609–292–6220

New Mexico
  Albuquerque Community Foundation
  6400 Uptown Boulevard N.E.
  Suite 500-W
  Albuquerque 87105
  505–883–6240

- New Mexico State Library
  325 Don Gaspar Street
  Santa Fe 87503
  505–827–3827

New York
- New York State Library
  Cultural Education Center
  Humanities Section
  Empire State Plaza
  Albany 12230
  518–473–4636

- Suffolk Cooperative Library System
  627 North Sunrise Service Road
  Bellport 11713
  516–286–1600

  New York Public Library
  Bronx Reference Center
  2556 Bainbridge Avenue
  Bronx 10458
  212–220–6575

Brooklyn in Touch
One Hanson Place
Room 2504
Brooklyn 11243
718–230–3200

- Buffalo and Erie County Public
Library
Lafayette Square
Buffalo 14202
716–858–7103

Huntington Public Library
338 Main Street
Huntington 11743
516–427–5165

Queens Borough Public Library
89-11 Merrick Boulevard
Jamaica 11432
718–990–0700

- Levittown Public Library
One Bluegrass Lane
Levittown 11756
516–731–5720

SUNY/College at Old Westbury
Library
223 Store Hill Road
Old Westbury 11568
516–876–3156

- Plattsburgh Public Library
15 Oak Street
Plattsburgh 12901
518–563–0921

Adriance Memorial Library
93 Market Street
Poughkeepsie 12601
914–485–3445

- Rochester Public Library
Business Division
115 South Avenue
Rochester 14604
716–428–7328

Staten Island Council on the Arts
One Edgewater Plaza, Rm. 311
Staten Island 10305
718–447–4485

- Onondaga County Public Library
at the Galleries
447 S. Salina Street
Syracuse 13202–2494
315–448–4636

- White Plains Public Library
100 Martine Avenue
White Plains 10601
914–682–4480

North Carolina
- Asheville-Buncomb Technical
Community College
Learning Resources Center
340 Victoria Rd.
Asheville 28802
704–254–1921 ext. 300

- The Duke Endowment
200 S. Tryon Street, Ste. 1100
Charlotte 28202
704–376–0291

Durham County Library
300 N. Roxboro Street
Durham 27702
919–560–0100

- North Carolina State Library
109 East Jones Street
Raleigh 27611
919–733–3270

- The Winston-Salem Foundation
229 First Union Bank Building
Winston-Salem 27101
919–725–2382

North Dakota
- North Dakota State University
The Library
Fargo 58105
701–237–8886

Ohio

Stark County District Library
715 Market Avenue North
Canton 44702–1080
216–452–0665

- Public Library of Cincinnati and
Hamilton County
Education Department
800 Vine Street
Cincinnati 45202–2071
513–369–6940

Columbus Metropolitan Library
96 S. Grant Avenue
Columbus 43215
614–645–2590

- Dayton and Montgomery County
Public Library
Grants Information Center
215 E. Third Street
Dayton 45402–2103
513–227–9500 ext. 211

- Toledo–Lucas County Public Library
Social Science Department
325 Michigan Street
Toledo 43623
419–259–5245

Ohio University–Zanesville
Community Education and Development
1425 Newark Road
Zanesville 43701
614–453–0762

Oklahoma

- Oklahoma City University Library
2501 North Blackwelder
Oklahoma City 73106
405–521–5072

- Tulsa City–County Library System
400 Civic Center
Tulsa 74103
918–596–7944

Oregon

- Pacific Non-Profit Network
Grantsmanship Resource Library
33 N. Central, Ste. 211
Medford 97501
503–779–6044

- Multnomah County Library
Government Documents Room
801 S.W. Tenth Avenue
Portland 97205–2597
503–223–7201

Oregon State Library
State Library Building
Salem 97310
503–378–4274

Pennsylvania

Northampton Community College
Learning Resources Center
3835 Green Pond Road
Bethlehem 18017
215–861–5360

- Erie County Public Library
3 South Perry Square
Erie 16501
814–451–6927

- Dauphin County Library System
101 Walnut Street
Harrisburg 17101
717–234–4961

Lancaster County Public Library
125 North Duke Street
Lancaster 17602
717–394–2651

- The Free Library of Philadelphia
Logan Square
Philadelphia 19103
215–686–5423

University of Pittsburgh
Hillman Library
Pittsburgh 15260
412–648–7722

Economic Development Council
of Northeastern Pennsylvania
1151 Oak Street
Pittston 18640
717–655–5581

Rhode Island
• Providence Public Library
  Reference Department
  150 Empire Street
  Providence 02903
  401–521–7722

South Carolina
• Charleston County Library
  404 King Street
  Charleston 29403
  803–723–1645

• South Carolina State Library
  Reference Department
  1500 Senate Street
  Columbia 29211
  803–734–8666

South Dakota
• South Dakota State Library
  800 Governors Drive
  Pierre 57501–2294
  605–773–5070
  800–592–1841 (SD residents)

  Sioux Falls Area Foundation
  141 N. Main Ave., Suite 500
  Sioux Falls 57102–1134
  605–336–7055

Tennessee
• Knoxville-Knox County Public
  Library
  500 West Church Avenue
  Knoxville 37902
  615–544–5750

• Memphis & Shelby County Public Library
  1850 Peabody Avenue
  Memphis 38104
  901–725–8877

• Public Library of Nashville and
  Davidson County
  8th Ave. N. and Union St.
  Nashville 37211
  615–259–6256

Texas
• Community Foundation of Abilene
  Funding Information Library
  708 NCNB Bldg.
  402 Cypress
  Abilene 79601
  915–676–3883

  Amarillo Area Foundation
  70 1st National Place 1
  800 S. Fillmore
  Amarillo 79101
  806–376–4521

  Hogg Foundation for Mental
  Health
  University of Texas
  Austin 78713
  512–471–5041

• Corpus Christi State University
  Library
  6300 Ocean Drive
  Corpus Christi 78412
  512–994–2608

• Dallas Public Library
  Grants Information Service
  1515 Young Street
  Dallas 75201
  214–670–1487

• Pan American University
  Learning Resource Center
  1201 W. University Drive
  Edinburg 78539
  512–381–3304

- El Paso Community Foundation
  1616 Texas Commerce Building
  El Paso 79901
  915–533–4020

- Texas Christian University Library
  Funding Information Center
  Ft. Worth 76129
  817–921–7664

- Houston Public Library
  Bibliographic Information Center
  500 McKinney Avenue
  Houston 77002
  713–236–1313

- Lubbock Area Foundation
  502 Texas Commerce Bank Building
  Lubbock 79401
  806–762–8061

- Funding Information Center
  507 Brooklyn
  San Antonio 78215
  512–227–4333

Utah
- Salt Lake City Public Library
  Business and Science Dept.
  209 East Fifth South
  Salt Lake City 84111
  801–363–5733

Vermont
- Vermont Dept. of Libraries
  Reference Services
  109 State Street
  Montpelier 05602
  802–828–3268

Virginia
- Hampton Public Library
  Grants Resources Collection
  4207 Victoria Blvd.
  Hampton 23669
  804–727–1154

- Richmond Public Library
  Business, Science, & Technology
  101 East Franklin Street
  Richmond 23219
  804–780–8223

- Roanoke City Public Library System
  Central Library
  706 S. Jefferson Street
  Roanoke 24014
  703–981–2477

Washington
- Seattle Public Library
  1000 Fourth Avenue
  Seattle 98104
  206–386–4620

- Spokane Public Library
  Funding Information Center
  West 906 Main Avenue
  Spokane 99201
  509–838–3364

West Virginia
- Kanawha County Public Library
  123 Capital Street
  Charleston 25304
  304–343–4646

Wisconsin
- University of Wisconsin—
  Madison
  Memorial Library
  728 State Street
  Madison 53706
  608–262–3242

- Marquette University Memorial Library
  1415 West Wisconsin Avenue
  Milwaukee 53233
  414–288–1515

Wyoming
- Laramie County Community College Library
1400 East College Drive
Cheyenne 82007–3299
307–778–1205

Australia
ANZ Executors & Trustees Co. Ltd.
91 William St., 7th Floor
Melbourne VIC 3000
03–648–5764

Canada
Canadian Centre for Philanthropy
74 Victoria Street, Suite 920
Toronto, Ontario M5C 2A5
416–368–1138

England
Charities Aid Foundation
18 Doughty Street
London WC1N 2PL
01–831–7798

Japan
Foundation Center Library of Japan
Elements Shinjuku Bldg. 3F
2-1-14 Shinjuku, Shinjuku-ku
Tokyo 160
03–350–1857

Mexico
Biblioteca Benjamin Franklin
American Embassy, USICA
Londres 16
Mexico City 6, D.F. 06600
905–211–0042

Puerto Rico
University of Puerto Rico
Ponce Technological College Library
Box 7186
Ponce 00732
809–844–4150

Universidad Del Sagrado Corazon
M.M.T. Guevarra Library
Correo Calle Loiza
Santurce 00914
809–728–1515 ext. 357

U.S. Virgin Islands
University of the Virgin Islands
Paiewonsky Library
Charlotte Amalie
St. Thomas 00802
809–828–3261

THE FOUNDATION CENTER AFFILIATES PROGRAM

As participants in the Cooperating Collections Network, affiliates are libraries or nonprofit agencies that provide fundraising information or other funding-related technical assistance in their communities. Affiliates agree to provide free public access to a basic collection of Foundation Center publications during a regular schedule of hours, offering free funding research guidance to all visitors. Many also provide a variety of special services for local nonprofit organizations using staff or volunteers to prepare special materials, organize workshops, or conduct library orientations.

The Foundation Center welcomes inquiries from agencies interested in providing this type of public information service. If you are interested in establishing a funding information library for the use of nonprofit agencies in your area, or in learning more about the program, we would like to hear from you. For more information, please write to: Anne J. Borland, The Foundation Center, 79 Fifth Avenue, New York, NY 10003.

Reprinted with permission from the Foundation Center, New York, NY, 1990.

APPENDIX C

Bibliography of State and Local Foundation Directories

Compiled and edited by

**Margaret Derrickson and Kevin Kurdylo,
Bibliographic Information Service**

*with assistance from
Oliver Smith and Elizabeth McKenty*

Alabama. *Alabama Foundation Directory*. Birmingham, Ala.: Birmingham Public Library, 1983. Based primarily on 1982 and 1983 990-PF returns filed with the IRS by 194 foundations. Main section arranged alphabetically by foundation; entries include areas of interest and officers, but no sample grants. Indexes of geographic areas and major areas of interest. Available from Reference Department, Birmingham Public Library, 2020 Park Place, Birmingham, AL 35203.

Alabama. Taylor, James H. *Foundation Profiles of the Southeast: Alabama, Arkansas, Louisiana, Mississippi*. Williamsburg, Ky.: James H. Taylor Associates, 1983. Based on 1978 and 1979 990-PF and 990-AR returns filed with the IRS by 212 foundations. Main section arranged by state and alphabetically by foundation name; entries include principal officer, assets, total grants and sample grants. No indexes. Available from James H. Taylor Associates, Inc., 804 Main Street, Williamsburg, KY 40769.

Alabama. See also **Tennessee:** O'Donnell, Suzanna, et al. *A Guide to Funders in Central Appalachia and the Tennessee Valley.*

Arizona. Junior League of Phoenix, comp. *Arizona Foundation Directory*. 2nd ed. Phoenix, Ariz.: Junior League of Phoenix, 1989. Profiles of more than 150 private and community foundations are featured in this directory produced by the Junior League of Phoenix in cooperation with the Arizona Chapter of the National Society of Fund Raising Executives. Includes foundations which have assets over $5,000 and which have made at least a total of $500 in grants. Descriptions include name, address, telephone number, source of information, employer identification number, year established, donors, purpose/fields of interest, restrictions, trustees, contact person, application deadline, and preferred form of contact. A presentation of financial data notes the fiscal year, total assets, total grants, number of grants, highest/lowest grants, and selected sample grants of the foundation. The directory also includes a guide for program planning, proposal writing, and budget formulation. Indexed by foundation name. Available from the Junior League of Phoenix, Inc., P.O. Box 10377, Phoenix, AZ 85064.

Arkansas. Cronin, Jerry. *1986 Guide to Arkansas Funding Sources.* West Memphis, Ark.: Independent Community Consultants, 1986. Contains information on 93 private Arkansas foundations, 59 corporate foundations, 33 scholarship sources, 26 church funding sources, and seven neighboring foundations (out-of-state foundations with Arkansas giving interests). Descriptions of the private and neighboring foundations include the name, address, phone number, employer ID number, contact, trustee(s), year-end financial information, notes, summary of grantmaking by giving area with sample grants, total dollars granted, number of grants made and grant range. Descriptions for other giving programs include the organization's name, address, phone number, contact person, preferred method of contact, application deadline and notes. Also included is a listing of inactive foundations. Available from Independent Community Consultants, Inc., Research & Evaluation Office, P.O. Box 1673, West Memphis, AR 72301.

Arkansas. See also **Alabama:** Taylor, James H. *Foundation Profiles of the Southeast; Alabama, Arkansas, Louisiana, Mississippi.*

California. Allen, Herb, and Sam Sternberg, eds. *Small Change from Big Bucks: A Report and Recommendations on Bay Area Foundations and Social Change.* San Francisco: Bay Area Committee for Responsive Philanthropy, 1979. Based primarily on 1976 990-AR returns filed with the IRS, CT-2 forms filed with California, annual reports, and interviews with 45 Bay Area foundations. Main section arranged alphabetically by foundation; entries include statement of purpose and contact person, but no sample grants. Also sections on the Bay Area Committee for Responsive Philanthropy, foundations and social change, the study methodology, the committee's findings, and the committee's recommendations. No indexes. Appendixes include Bay Area resources for technical assistance, bibliography, nonprofit organizations in law and fact, and glossary. Available from Bay

Area Committee for Responsive Philanthropy, 944 Market St., San Francisco, CA 94102.

California. Fanning, Carol. *Guide to California Foundations.* 7th ed. San Francisco: Northern California Grantmakers, 1988. This directory lists more than 800 foundations located in California which award grants totaling $40,000 or more annually. Based primarily on 990-PF returns filed with the IRS or records in the California Attorney General's Office; some additional data supplied by foundations completing questionnaires. Main section arranged alphabetically by foundation; entries include statement of purpose, sample grants, and officers. Also section on applying for grants. Indexes of all foundations by name, subject, and county location. Available from Northern California Grantmakers, 116 New Montgomery Street, Suite 742, San Francisco, CA 94105. (415) 777-5761.

California. Ford, Gerald, Leslye Louie, and David Miller. *An Examination of Bay Area Corporate Non-Cash Contributions: Programs and policies for the Eighties.* San Francisco: Coro Foundation, 1981. Examines corporate non-cash contributions and selected creative projects. Model programs are described to encourage other companies to broaden their own contributions programs. Provides strategies for non-profits seeking non-cash contributions, with profiles of 38 corporate contribution programs in the San Francisco Bay Area. Profiles include contact, assets, number of employees, types of non-cash contributions, and program emphasis. Appendix is a cross-reference list of corporate non-cash contribution programs by type. Available from Coro Foundation, 609 S. Grant Street, #810, Los Angeles, CA 90017.

California. Logos Associates. *The Directory of the Major California Foundations.* Attleboro, Mass: Logos Associates, 1986. Based on 1983 and 1984 990-PF returns and annual reports for more than 97 foundations. Main section arranged alphabetically by foundation; entries include contact person, activities, categories of giving, board meeting dates, officers and directors, and grants (coded to show type of aid). Subject index. Available from Logos Associates, 7 Park Street, Rm. 212. Attleboro, MA 02703.

California. *San Diego County Foundation Directory.* San Diego, Calif.: San Diego Community Foundation, 1989. Based on 990-PF returns filed with the IRS for 67 foundations and 56 corporations. Main sections arranged alphabetically. Entries include contact person, type of support, range of grants, total amount and number of grants, application procedures and directors; no date of financial information indicated. No indexes. Available from San Diego Community

Foundation, 525 "B" Street, Suite 410, San Diego, CA 92101. (619) 239-8815.

California. Santa Clara County Office of Education. *Corporate Contributions Guide to Santa Clara County.* San Jose, Calif.: Grantsmanship Resource Center [1989]. Directory of 266 corporations in Santa Clara County (Silicon Valley). Entries vary in completeness; provide address, contact person and phone number, designation for type of office, indication of whether or not the company has a contribution program preferred program areas, application guidelines, contribution finances, non-cash contributions, and matching gift programs. Indexed by areas of interest. Available from The Nonprofit Development Center, 1762 Technology Drive, Suite 225, San Jose, CA 95110. (408) 452-8181.

Connecticut. Burns, Michael E., ed. *Connecticut Foundation Directory.* Hartford, Conn.: D.A.T.A., 1987. Based on 1986 and 1987 990-PF forms filed with the Connecticut Attorney General's Office and completed questionnaires from a December 1987, survey of more than 900 foundations. Main section arranged alphabetically by foundation; entries include selected grants list, principal officer, and purpose statement. Index of foundations by city and an alphabetical index. Available from D.A.T.A., Inc., 30 Arbor St. North, Hartford, CT 06106. (203) 786-5225.

Connecticut. Burns, Michael E., ed. *Guide to Corporate Giving in Connecticut.* Hartford, Conn.: D.A.T.A., 1986. Features alphabetical and geographic listings of more than 850 corporations; specific information for local Connecticut users; names, titles, and roles of charitable giving contacts; foundation information; non-cash giving policies; matching gift policies and priorities; and cash giving policies, procedures and priorities. Available from D.A.T.A. see above.

Connecticut. Logos Associates, comp. *Directory of the Major Connecticut Foundations.* Attleboro, Mass.: Logos Associates, 1982. Based on 1979 through 1980 990-PF and 990-AR returns, foundation publications and information from the Office of the Attorney General in Hartford. Sixty-one foundations arranged alphabetically; entries include grant range, sample grants, geographic limitations, officers and directors. Index of subjects. Available from Logos Associates, 7 Park St., Rm. 212, Attleboro, MA 02703.

Colorado. *Colorado Foundation Directory.* 6th ed. Denver, Colo.: Junior League of Denver, 1988. Information on more than 170 foundations, covering fiscal years from 1984 through 1987; entries include purpose statement/field of interest, sample grants, and contacts. Also includes an excellent guide to program planning and proposal writing.

Indexed by areas of foundation interest. Available from Junior League of Denver, Inc., 6300 East Yale Avenue, Denver, CO 80222. (303) 692-0270.

Delaware. United Way of Delaware. *Delaware Foundations.* Wilmington, Del.: United Way of Delaware, 1983. Based on 1979 through 1981 990-PF and 990-AR returns filed with the IRS, annual reports, and information supplied by 154 foundations. Main section arranged alphabetically by foundation; entries include statement of purpose and officers, grant analysis, type of recipient; no sample grants. Detailed information on 111 private foundations, a list of 27 operating foundations and a sampling of out-of-state foundations with a pattern of giving in Delaware. Alphabetical index of foundation names and index of all trustees and officers. Available from United Way of Delaware, Inc., 701 Shipley St., Wilmington, DE 19801. (302) 573-2414.

District of Columbia. Community Foundation of Greater Washington. *Directory of Foundations of the Greater Washington Area.* Washington, D.C.: Community Foundation of Greater Washington, 1988. Biennial directory of public and private foundations and trusts as well as some corporate foundations in the greater Washington area. Directory is divided into two sections. Section 1 contains the larger foundations with assets of $1 million or more, or which made grants of $100,000 or more in the reported years, and Section 2 lists the smaller foundations which have below $1 million in assets, or awarded grants of less than $100,000. Section 2 comprises the largest number of foundations. Four indexes include: an alphabetical index of foundations; an alphabetical index of trustees, directors, and managers; an index of foundations in order of the size of their assets; and an index grouped by the specific area of interest. Information on each foundation includes: name and address; telephone number; contact person, trustees, directors, and managers; areas of interest; application guidelines; financial and grant data (total assets, number of grants, amount of grants, grant range, and the five largest grants). Preceding the directory are helpful statistical tables and lists for distribution of giving by foundation asset size, and by amount of grants awarded, largest independent/family foundations by total giving, largest company-sponsored foundations by total giving, community foundations by total giving, 15 largest grants, foundations not included in the directory, and foundations that do not accept proposals. Also included is a brief adaptation of F. Lee and Barbara L. Jacquette's, "What makes a good proposal?" Available from Community Foundation of Greater Washington, Inc., 1002 Wisconsin Ave., N.W., Washington, DC 20007. (202) 338-8993.

Florida. Kruse, J. Carol, ed. *The Complete Guide to Florida Foun-*

dations. 2nd ed. Miami, Fla.: John L. Adams and Co., 1988. Based primarily on information contained in 990-PF returns for more than 1,000 foundations. Main section arranged alphabetically by foundation name; entries include officers, assets, total grants amount, range of grant amounts, funding priorities, and geographic preferences. Indexed by county and foundation funding priorities. Also includes an index of foundations excluded from the "Guide." Available from John L. Adams & Co. Inc., P.O. Box 561565, Miami, FL 33256-1565.

Florida. Logos Associates, *The Directory of the Major Florida Foundations.* Attleboro, Mass.: Logos Associates, 1987. Profiles 107 major Florida foundations that made more than $50,000 in grants in 1984. Entries include information on contact person, foundation activities, financial data, officers and directors, geographic range, and grants made. Address, telephone number, contact person, and officers are given for 775 foundations making grants of less than $50,000. Includes subject index. Available from Logos Associates, see above.

Georgia. Taylor, James H. Foundation *Profiles of the Southeast: Georgia.* Williamsburg, Ky.: James H. Taylor Associates, 1983. Based on 1975 through 1977 990-PF and 990-AR returns filed with the IRS for 530 foundations. Main section arranged alphabetically by foundation; entries include statement of purpose, sample grants, and principal officer. Indexes of foundation names, cities, and program interests. Available from James H. Taylor Assoc., Inc., 804 Main St., Williamsburg, KY 40769.

Georgia. See also **Tennessee:** O'Donnell, Suzanna, et al. *A Guide to Funders in Central Appalachia and the Tennessee Valley.* Available from Appalachian Community Fund, 517 Union St., Suite 206, Knoxville, TN 37902.

Hawaii. Alu Like. *A Guide to Charitable Trusts and Foundations in the State of Hawaii.* Honolulu, Hawaii: Alu Like, 1984, Part 1 provides sample forms for forming a tax-exempt organization in the state of Hawaii and with the Internal Revenue Service, as well as a reprint of "Program Planning and Proposal Writing" by Norton J. Kiritz. Part 2 provides information on 72 charitable trusts and foundations in Hawaii (detail of information varies), brief information on 16 mainland foundations with sample grants made in Hawaii, profiles for 11 national church funding sources, and a listing of local resource service organizations. Brief bibliography. Indexed by organization. Available from Alu Like, 401 Kamakee St., 3rd fl., Honolulu, HI 96814. (808) 521-9571.

Hawaii. Thompson, Susan A., comp. *Foundation Grants in Ha-*

waii, 1970–1980: Grants Awarded by Mainland Foundations to Recipients in the State of Hawaii. Honolulu, Hawaii: University of Hawaii at Manoa Libraries, 1981. Foundation grants made to recipients in Hawaii, arranged by state. Indexed by recipients and subject categories. Includes addresses for foundations. Selected bibliography. Available from University of Hawaii at Manoa, Libraries, General Reference Dept.

Idaho. *Directory of Idaho Foundations.* 4th ed. Caldwell, Idaho; Caldwell Public Library, 1988. Based on 1986 990-PF returns filed with the IRS and questionnaires answered by 100 foundations. Arranged in four sections: (1) active foundations that accept applications, (2) scholarship-granting foundations, (3) foundations that do not accept applications or appear to be inactive and, (4) national and corporate giving in Idaho. Entries vary in completeness, containing information on assets, grants paid, range of grants, sample grants, and application information. Alphabetical index. Available from Caldwell Public Library, 1010 Dearborn St., Caldwell, ID 83605-4195. (208) 459-3242.

Illinois. Capriotti, Beatrice J., and Frank J. Capriotti, eds. *Illinois Foundation Directory.* Minneapolis, Minn.: Foundation Data Center. Profiles of approximately 1,900 foundations based on 990-PF and 990-AR returns filed with the IRS and information received from questionnaires. Main section arranged alphabetically by foundation; entries include financial data, statement and purpose, listing of all grants, officers, and principal contributors. Index section contains a summary report of foundations with special purpose or assets under $200,000; banks/trusts as corporate trustees; donors, trustees, and administrators; survey of foundation interests; and foundation guidelines and deadlines. Updated quarterly. Available from Foundation Data Center, 401 Kenmar Circle, Minnetonka, MN 55343. (612) 542-8582.

Illinois. Dick, Ellen A. *Chicago's Corporate Foundations: A Directory of Chicago Area and Illinois Corporate Foundations.* Oak Park, Ill.: Ellen Dick, 1988. Entries for 122 corporate foundations provide contact person, phone number, area of giving and limitations, deadlines, total assets, total grants, high/low grant amounts, officers, and the major products or services of the parent corporations. Index of in-kind contributions, areas of giving, and matching gift programs. Available from Ellen Dick, 838 Fair Oaks, Oak Park, IL 60302. (312) 386-9385.

Illinois. Donors Forum of Chicago. *The Directory of Illinois Foundations.* Chicago: Donors Forum of Chicago, 1986. Alphabetically arranged directory provides information on more than 400 Illinois foundations and trusts. The directory is arranged into four main sections: foundations, analysis section, subject index, and county index. Foundation listings give: foundation name, telephone number, contact name, donor type, purpose, field of interest, program limitations, geographic limits, contact procedure, information available, funding cycle, application deadlines, paid staff, matching gifts, grants to government funded agencies or programs, total assets, total grants, number of grants, grant range, model grant, officers and directors. The analysis section contains a synthesis of the statistical data collected for the directory. Graphs and charts are included in addition to a breakdown of the 400 foundations by type—family, corporate, community, independent, or operating. The volume contains both county and subject indexes. The "County Index" contains a foundation listing and a compilation of total assets and grants made for each county and city. The "Subject Index" contains foundation listings by broad subject categories. Available from Donors Forum of Chicago, 53 W. Jackson St., Suite 430, Chicago, IL 60604. (314) 431-0260.

Illinois. Donors Forum of Chicago. *Members Grants List.* Chicago: Donors Forum of Chicago, 1988. A product of the Donors Forum of Chicago's Philanthropic Database Project, this list represents grants of $500 or more awarded by 54 Donors Forum members to organizations within the Chicago Metropolitan Area. Grantmakers arranged alphabetically; grants are arranged under subject areas showing the name and state of the donee, the specific purpose of the grant within broad subject areas, the type of support, coded descriptions of the beneficiary group, and the amount of the grant. Supplies only the name and address of the grantmaking organizations. Grants are arranged by donor organization and by recipient organization; index of donor organizations by grant purpose. Appendixes list the 50 largest recipient organizations, percentage of grants by broad subject of grant purpose, percentage of grants by purpose code within the broad subject areas, and percentage of grants by type of support. Available from Donors Forum, see above.

Illinois. Sheck, Diane, comp. *Members and Library Partners Directory.* Chicago: Donors Forum of Chicago, 1988. Provides data on 145 Donors Forum member foundations and corporate contributions programs. When provided, information includes principal funding areas, total assets (applicable only to foundations), total grants, fiscal year, percentage of grants in greater Chicago and outside Illinois, number of board members, frequency of meetings, names of professional staff, and whether or not guidelines and annual reports are available, or if an employee matching gifts program exists (applicable for corporate contributions programs). Two tables rank the 50 largest Donors

Forum foundation members based on total assets and the 50 largest Donors Forum member organizations based on total grants. Available from Donors Forum, see above.

Indiana. Indiana Donors Alliance. *Directory of Indiana Donors.* Indianapolis, Ind.: Indiana Donors Alliance, 1989. Contains profiles of 475 active grantmaking foundations, trusts, and scholarship programs in Indiana. Arranged alphabetically, each profile includes the donor's name and IRS identification number; the name, address, and telephone number of a contact person; recent financial data (assets, grants paid, number of grants made, and the range of grants); eligibility for grants; program interests, geographic preferences; limitations; and application procedure. The appendix contains graphs showing the number of donors within broad ranges of giving and the amount of grants paid per ranges of giving. The donor profiles are indexed by grants paid (ranked highest to lowest, all foundations having made at least $2,000 in grants), by program interests, and by county. A map shows the number of donors by county. Available from Indiana Donors Alliance, 1500 North Delaware Street, Indianapolis, IN 46202. (317) 638-1500.

Indiana. Spear, Paula Reading, ed. *Indiana Foundations: A Directory.* Indianapolis, Ind.: Central Research Systems, 1985. Based on 1983 and 1984 990-PF returns filed with the IRS and information supplied by 288 foundations. Main section arranged alphabetically by foundation; entries include officers, areas of interest, sample grants, high and low grants. Indexes of financial criteria, subjects, counties, and officers. Appendixes of restricted foundations, foundations for student assistance only, and foundations without funding. Available from Central Research Systems, 320 N. Meridian, Suite 515, Indianapolis, IN 46204.

Iowa. Holm, Diana M. *Iowa Directory of Foundations.* Dubuque, Iowa: Trumpet Associates, 1984. Based primarily on returns filed with the IRS and information supplied by 247 foundations; date of information is 1982 in most cases, no date is given in other entries. Main section arranged alphabetically by foundation; most entries include address, telephone number, Employer Identification Number, total assets, total grants, purpose and activities, officers and trustees, and contact person. Appendix of cancelled foundations. Indexed by city. Available from Trumpet Assoc., Inc., P.O. Box 172, Dubuque, IA 52001. (319) 582-3153.

Kansas. Rhodes, James H., ed. *The Directory of Kansas Foundations.* Topeka, Kans.: Topeka Public Library, 1989. More than 300 foundations and trusts are featured in this new edition. Information was gathered from public records, Kansas Attorney General files, and questionnaire responses. Each profile notes the grantmaker's name; address; phone number; financial data (assets, total annual gifts, high/ low gift, number of gifts, and date of data); board members; funding priority areas, including types of support and sample grants; limitations; application information; and additional information. Contains a bibliography of various materials designed to aid the grantseeker; the front matter of the directory discusses composing a proposal. Indexes are arranged alphabetically by foundation name, city, and subject area. Available from Topeka Public Library Foundation Center Collection, 1515 West Tenth Street, Topeka, KS 66604. (913) 233-2040.

Kentucky. Dougherty, Nancy C., ed. *A Guide to Kentucky Grantmakers.* Louisville, Ky.: Louisville Foundation, 1982. Based on questionnaires to 101 foundations and their 1981 990-PF and 990-AR IRS returns. Arranged alphabetically by foundation; entries include assets, total grants paid, number of grants, smallest/largest grant, primary area of interest, and contact person. No indexes. Available from The Louisville Foundation, Inc., 623 W. Main St., Louisville, KY 40202. (502) 585-4649.

Kentucky. Taylor, James J., and John L. Wilson. *Foundation Profiles of the Southeast: Kentucky, Tennessee, Virginia.* Williamsburg, Ky.: James H. Taylor Associates, 1981. Based on 1978 and 1979 990-PF and 990-AR IRS returns for 117 foundations. Main section arranged alphabetically by foundation; entries include assets, total number and amount of grants, sample grants, and officers. No indexes. Available from James H. Taylor Associates, Inc., 804 Main St., Williamsburg, KY 40769.

Kentucky. See also **Tennessee:** O'Donnell, Suzanna, et al. *A Guide to Funders in Central Appalachia and the Tennessee Valley.*

Louisiana. Lazaro, Joseph A., comp. *Citizens' Handbook of Private Foundations in New Orleans, Louisiana.* New Orleans, La.: Greater New Orleans Foundation, 1987. Directory of 112 foundations located and making grants in New Orleans, Louisiana. Data are taken from IRS 990-PF forms filed for 1985. Entries provide information on foundation purpose; contact person; phone number; officers, managers, and trustees; special notations; and financial data (net worth, grant recipients and amounts awarded, and total number and amount of grants awarded). Appendixes include statistics on private philanthropy, resources for grantseekers at the New Orleans Public Library, information reprinted from the Foundation Center, a sample IRS 990-PF form, a listing of private foundations located in the state of Louisiana reprinted from the Foundation Center's "National Data Book," tips on grantsmanship, a foundation prospect worksheet, and a glossary. No indexes. Available from The Greater New Orleans Foundation, 2515 Canal St., Suite 401, New Orleans, LA 70119 (504) 822-4906.

Louisiana. See also **Alabama:** Taylor, James H. *Foundation Profiles of the Southeast: Alabama, Arkansas, Louisiana, Mississippi.*

Maine. Brysh, Janet F., ed. *Maine Corporate Foundation Directory.* Portland, Maine: University of Southern Maine, 1984. Based on information supplied by approximately 75 corporations. Main section arranged alphabetically by corporation; entries include contact person and, for a few corporations, the areas of interest. Alphabetical index. Available from University of Southern Maine, Office of Sponsored Research, 246 Deering Ave., Room 628, Portland, ME 04103. (207) 780-4871.

Maine. Burns, Michael E., ed. *Corporate Philanthropy in New England: Maine.* Vol 3. Hartford, Conn.: D.A.T.A., 1987. Entries for more than 180 corporate giving programs, providing address, phone number, and contact, brief corporate profile, general philanthropic policies, annual cash contributions, and giving priorities and interests. Subject and geographic indexes. Available from D.A.T.A., see above.

Maine. Office of Sponsored Research. *Directory of Maine Foundations.* 7th ed., rev. Portland, Maine: University of Southern Maine, 1988. Based on information compiled from foundations, the Foundation Center, and primarily 990-PF returns filed with the IRS. Lists more than 62 Maine foundations having assets from $799 to $7,024,391. Entries include contact person, number of grants awarded, total amount awarded, and sample grants. Also includes a section with feasibility study to be conducted prior to proposal development and/or fundraising, a self-evaluation, a fundraising intelligence test, and a suggested grant request outline. Entries are arranged alphabetically under cities and towns; indexed alphabetically. Available from University of Southern Maine, Office of Sponsored Research, see above.

Maryland. Maryland Attorney General's Office. *Annual Index of Foundation Reports and Appendix, 1987.* Baltimore, Md.: Attorney General's Office, 1989. Information on 443 foundations compiled from 1987 IRS 990-PF forms filed with the Maryland Attorney General's office (appendix contains information on 60 foundations which filed after December 1, 1988). The index and appendix are arranged alphabetically; entries give the foundation's name, address, telephone number, employer identification number, fair market value of the foundation, foundation managers and their addresses, purpose of contributions, contact person, contributions given during the fiscal year with the recipient and amount, total contributions given during the fiscal year, and contributions approved for future payment, if any. Available from the Attorney General, 7 North Calvert St., Baltimore, MD 21202. (301) 576-6300.

Massachusetts. Associated Grantmakers of Massachusetts. *Massachusetts Grantmakers.* Boston: Associated Grantmaker of Massachusetts, 1990. Published at the request of the Massachusetts Attorney General, this directory contains descriptions of 438 foundations and corporate grantmakers in Massachusetts. Entries indicate type of grantmaking organization, whether support is given to nonprofit organizations and/or individuals, grantmaking philosophy and program emphasis, program interests, geographic focus, financial information, application procedures, trustees, and contact person. A reference chart indexing grantmaking organizations according to program areas and population groups is included. Index to geographic locations and sources of individual support. Foundation Center collections in New England, and those operated by the Foundation Center. Available from Associated Grantmakers of Mass., Inc. 294 Washington St., Suite 840, Boston, MA 02108. (617) 426-2606.

Massachusetts. Burns, Michael E., ed. *Guide to Corporate Giving in Massachusetts.* Hartford, Conn.: D.A.T.A., 1983. Based on questionnaires and telephone interviews reaching 737 corporations. Main section arranged alphabetically by city and zip code; entries include product, amount given annually, frequency, area of interest, and non-cash contributions. Index of corporations by city. Available from D.A.T.A., see above.

Massachusetts. Logos Associates, comp. *Directory of the Major Greater Boston Foundations,* Attleboro, Mass.: Logos Associates, 1981. Based on 1975 through 1980 990-PF and 990-AR returns filed with the IRS by 56 Boston area foundations. Main section arranged alphabetically by foundation; entries include statement of purpose, sample grants, and officers. Indexed by fields of interest. Available from Logos, see above.

Massachusetts. Department of the Attorney General. *Directory of Foundations in Massachusetts.* Boston: Massachusetts Department of the Attorney General, 1977. Arranged in two sections, Part 1 lists 623 foundations which make grants (of $1,000 or more) primarily to organizations. Part 2 lists 411 foundations which make grants (of any amount) primarily to individuals. Entries in both sections provide address, telephone number, officers, trustees, finances (including assets, total expenditures, total grants, largest and smallest grant, and number of grants for the reported year), interests, restrictions, and purpose.

Part 1 includes appendixes which group foundations by the range of total grants made, by geographic restrictions, and by purposes. Appendixes in Part 2 list foundations which make loans to individuals, which give scholarships to individuals in particular geographic areas, which give scholarships to certain population groups, and which give scholarships according to a particular area of study. Available from Department of the Attorney General, State House, Boston, MA.

Massachusetts. Social Service Planning Corporation. *Private Sector Giving, Greater Worcester Area: A Directory and Index.* Worcester, Mass.: Social Service Planning Corp., 1987. 100 foundations arranged alphabetically; entries include financial data, contact person, and a listing of award recipients with the dollar amount each received. Categorical index chart gives access to the foundation entries by their funding interest. Available from The Social Service Planning Corporation.

Michigan. Fischer, Jeri L., ed. *The Michigan Foundation Directory.* 6th ed. Grand Haven, Mich.: Council of Michigan Foundations, 1988. Identifies more than 543 potential grantmaking sources in Michigan; this includes 475 foundations and 68 corporate giving programs. Divided into five separate parts: (1) largest foundations with assets of $200,000 or grantmaking of $25,000; (2) special purpose foundations (those with a single purpose); (3) foundations with assets less than $200,000 or grantmaking less than $25,000; (4) a listing of foundations by city; and (5) a listing of terminated foundations. Information about the largest foundations, special purpose foundations, and corporate foundations/giving programs in Section 2 includes address, phone number, contact person, donors, purpose and activities, geographic priorities, assets, expenditures, grant amounts, grant ranges, officers and trustees. Also presented is a comparison of the total number of grants and grant amounts made against those made in Michigan. Section 3 contains an in-depth analysis of grantmaking in Michigan. Section 4 provides information on how to research a foundation and compose grant proposals. The directory has indexes by subject, trustees, and foundation name. Available from Michigan League for Human Services, 300 N., Washington Square, Suite 401, Lansing, MI 48933. (517) 487-5436.

Michigan. Logos Associates, comp. *The Directory of the Major Michigan Foundations.* 2nd ed. Attleboro, Mass.: Logos Associates, 1989. Based on IRS financial data and most current annual reports, profiles in this directory offer in-depth information for more than 350 corporate and private foundations in Michigan. Excellent descriptions of foundation activities, program interests and past grants in addition to address, contact person, trustees, application information, and financial assets. Divided into sections for "Foundations Making Grants of $400,000 or More," "Major Michigan Corporations," "Foundations Making Grants From $101,000 to $399,999," and "Foundations Making Grants From $50,000 to $100,000." Indexed by foundation name, geographical location, and support interest. Available from Logos, see above.

Minnesota. Capriotti, Beatrice J., and Frank J. Capriotti, eds. *Minnesota Foundation Directory.* Minneapolis, Minn.: Foundation Data Center, 1985. Profiles on approximately 700 foundations based on 990-PF and 990-AR returns filed with the IRS plus returned questionnaires. Main section arranged alphabetically by foundation; entries include financial data, statement and purpose, listing of all grants, officers, and principal contributors. Index section contains a summary report of foundations with special purpose or assets under $200,000; banks/trusts as corporate trustees; donors, trustees and administrators; survey of foundation interests; and foundation guidelines and deadlines.

Minnesota. Minnesota Council on Foundations. *Guide to Minnesota Foundations and Corporate Giving Programs.* Minneapolis, Minn.: University of Minnesota Press, 1989. Based primarily on 1987 and 1988 IRS 990-PF returns and a survey of more than 600 grantmakers. Main section arranged alphabetically by foundation name; entries include program interests, officers and directors, assets, total grants, number of grants, range, and sample grants. Some entries include geographic orientation, types of organizations funded and types of support. Appendixes of inactive foundations, foundations with designated recipients, foundations making grants only outside of Minnesota, and foundations not accepting applications. Also section on funding research in Minnesota. Indexed by foundation name, types of organizations funded, and grantmakers by size (according to grants paid). Available from Minnesota Council on Foundations, 425 Peavey Bldg., 730 Second Ave. So., Minneapolis, MN 55402. (612) 338-1989.

Minnesota. Minnesota Council of Nonprofits. *Minnesota Foundations Sourcebook.* Minneapolis, Minn.: Minnesota Council of Nonprofits, 1989. Using data from "Minnesota Philanthropic Support for the Disadvantaged," profiles in this directory provide name, address, telephone number, contact person, and deadlines for the 60 largest Minnesota foundations and corporate giving programs. For some grantmakers additional information is provided, including percentage of total giving granted to benefit the disadvantaged, geographic distribution, grantee types, percentage between general support and project-related grants, a list of sample grants, the average percentage of the dollar amount requested that was actually granted, and a ratio of the methods of contact with staff (phone conversations, meetings, site visits). Arranged alphabetically, no indexes. Available from Minnesota Council of Nonprofits, 2700 University Ave. W., #250, St. Paul, MN 55514. (612) 642-1904.

Mississippi. See **Tennessee:** O'Donnell, Suzanna, et al. *A Guide to Funders in Central Appalachia and the Tennessee Valley.*

Mississippi. See also **Alabama:** Taylor, James H. *Foundation Profiles of the Southeast; Alabama, Arkansas, Louisiana, Mississippi.*

Missouri. Clearinghouse for Midcontinent Foundations, comp. *The Directory of Greater Kansas City Foundations.* Kansas City, Mo.: Clearinghouse for Midcontinent Foundations, 1986. Directory provides detailed profiles on 281 foundations and trusts in the eight-county Greater Kansas City (Missouri) metropolitan area. These foundations have estimated market assets of $610.5 million and estimated annual contributions of $37 million. The foundation listings, arranged alphabetically by foundation name, are indexed by broad fields of interest. The foundation profile contains the foundation name, address, telephone number, contact person, officers and directors, administrators, assets, fiscal year date, recipient information, range, limitations, purpose, and other information. Indexes included in the directory are "Top Twenty Grantmaking Foundations," based on assets; "Top Twenty Grantmaking Foundations," based on charitable payout; "Foundations with Designated Recipients"; and "Foundations Making Grants in (specific subject areas such as arts, health, etc.)." Available from The Clearinghouse for Midcontinent Foundations, P.O. Box 22680, Kansas City, MO 64113. (816) 276-1176.

Missouri. Swift, Wilda H., comp. and ed. *The Directory of Missouri Foundations.* 2nd ed. St. Louis, Mo.: Swift Associates, 1988. Based on 1986 and 1987 990-PF returns and questionnaires of 919 foundations. Included are sections on foundations making grants to organizations (large foundations, community foundations, and small foundations), foundations giving assistance to individuals (financial assistance to students and assistance to individuals in need), foundations with designated recipients, foundations which contribute scholarship funds to educational institutions, and inactive, operating, relocated, and terminated foundations. Entries include address, telephone number, contact person, assets, total grants amount, low and high grant amounts, and funding priorities. The directory includes alphabetical indexes by city and by foundation name. Available from Swift Associates, P.O. Box 28033, St. Louis, MO 63119.

Montana. McRae, Kendall, and Kim Pederson, eds. *The Montana and Wyoming Foundation Directory.* 4th ed. Billings, Mont.: Grants Assistance Center, 1986. Based on 990-PF returns filed with the IRS, the "National Data Book," and information supplied by 65 foundations in Montana and 20 in Wyoming. Main section arranged alphabetically by foundation; entries include areas of interest, geographic preference, application process, and contact person; no sample grants. Indexes of foundation names and areas of interest. Available from Eastern Montana College Library, 1500 North 30th, Billings, MT 59101. (406) 657-1666.

Nebraska. *Nebraska Foundation Directory.* Omaha, Nebr.: Junior League of Omaha, 1985. Based on mostly 1982 and 1983 990-PF returns filed with the IRS by approximately 200 foundations. Main section arranged alphabetically by foundation; entries include statement of purpose and officers. No sample grants or indexes. Available from Junior League of Omaha, 808 South 74th Plaza, Omaha, NE 68114.

Nevada. Honsa, Vlasta, comp. *Nevada Foundation Directory.* 2nd ed. Las Vegas, Nev.: Las Vegas-Clark County Library District, 1989. Based on 1987 and 1988 990-PF returns filed with the IRS and questionnaires completed by foundations and corporations. Main section arranged alphabetically by foundation or corporation name; entries include contact person, financial data, funding interests, and sample grants. Section on inactive and defunct Nevada foundations. Section on 42 national foundations that fund Nevada projects. Indexed by fields of interest, geographic location, and name. Available from Las Vegas-Clark County Library District, 1401 E. Flamingo Road, Las Vegas, NV 89119. (702) 733-7810.

New Hampshire. Burns, Michael E., ed. *Corporate Philanthropy in New England: New Hampshire 1987–1988.* New Haven, Conn.: DATA, 1987. Based on questionnaires answered by 275 corporations. Main section arranged alphabetically by corporation; entries include contact person, products, and giving interests. Subject index and list of corporations by city. Available from DATA, Inc., 30 Astor St. North, Hartford, CT 06106. (203) 786-5225.

New Hampshire. Office of the Attorney General. *Directory of Charitable Funds in New Hampshire.* 4th ed. Concord, N.H.: New Hampshire Office of the Attorney General, 1988. Based on records in the New Hampshire Attorney General's Office, and updated annually; published in June; 233 foundations arranged alphabetically; entries include statement of purpose, officers, and assets; no sample grants. Indexes of geographical areas when restricted, and of purposes when not geographically restricted. Grants for scholarships also included. Available from Division of Charitable Trusts, Office of the Attorney General, State House Annex, 23 Capitol St., Concord, NH 03301. (603) 271-3591.

New Jersey. Littman, Wendy P., ed. *The Mitchell Guide to Foundations, Corporations, and Their Managers; New Jersey.* Belle Mead, N.J.: Littman Associates, 1988. Based primarily on 990-PF returns filed with the IRS from 1984 through 1987 and, in some cases, information supplied by 196 foundations; data for the 558 companies on the corporation list compiled from basic business references. The funder profiles are arranged alphabetically by foundation name; entries include sample grants and foundation managers, restrictions and program priorities. The corporate section is a list which includes address, telephone, and contact person. Contains indexes by county for both foundations and corporations. Available from The Mitchell Guide, P.O. Box 613, Belle Mead, NJ 08502.

New Jersey. Logos Associates. *The Directory of the Major New Jersey Foundations.* Attleboro, Mass.: Logos Associates, 1988. Based on IRS financial data, annual reports, and other public materials; offers profiles on approximately 110 foundations, all of which have given away a minimum of $50,000 in the year of record, have distributed the bulk of this within the state of New Jersey, and are a source of funding to the general nonprofit institutions in New Jersey. Arranged alphabetically by foundation; entries include address, telephone number, contact, foundation activities, total assets and grants, information relevant to corporate foundations, officers and directors, and sample grants. Subject index. Available from Logos Associates, 7 Park St., Room 212, Attleboro, MA 02803.

New Mexico. Murrell, William G., and William M. Miller. *New Mexico Private Foundation Directory.* Tijeras, NM; New Moon Consultants, 1982. Thirty-five foundations and 17 corporations. Entries include contact person, program purpose, areas of interest, financial data, application procedure, meeting times, and publications. Also sections on proposal writing, private and corporate grantsmanship, library support and other information services, and bibliography. No indexes. Available from New Moon Consultants, P.O. Box 532, Tijeras, NM 87059.

New York. Mitchell, Rowland L., Jr., ed. *The Mitchell Guide to Foundations, Corporations and Their Managers: Central New York, Including Binghamton, Corning, Elmira, Geneva, Ithaca, Oswego, Syracuse, Utica.* 2nd ed. Scarsdale, N.Y.: Rowland Mitchell, Jr., 1987. Based on 990-PF returns filed with the IRS. Main sections arranged alphabetically by foundations which made grants totaling more than

$5,000 or had assets of $100,000 or more and by corporations with net earnings of at least $10 million. Entries for more than 90 foundations provide names of managers, financial data, and sample grants. Entries for more than 100 corporations provide address, phone number, names and titles of one or two executive officers, and the company's business focus. Alphabetical indexes of foundation and company names, as well as an index to managers. Available from Rowland L. Mitchell, Jr., Box 172, Scarsdale, NY 10583. (914) 723-7770.

New York. Mitchell, Rowland L., Jr., ed. *The Mitchell Guide to Foundations, Corporations and Their Managers: Long Island, Including Nassau and Suffolk Counties.* 2nd ed. Scarsdale, N.Y.: Rowland Mitchell, Jr., 1987. Based on 990-PF returns filed with the IRS. Main sections arranged alphabetically by foundations which made grants totaling more than $5,000 or had assets of $100,000 or more and by corporations with net earnings of at least $10 million. Entries for 180 foundations provide names of managers, financial data, and sample grants. Entries for 130 corporations provide address, phone number, the names and titles of one or two executive officers, and the company's business focus. Alphabetical indexes of foundation and corporation names, as well as an index to managers. Available from Rowland L. Mitchell, see above.

New York. Mitchell, Rowland L., Jr., ed. *The Mitchell Guide to Foundations, Corporations and Their Managers: Upper Hudson Valley Including Capital Area, Glens Falls, Newburgh, Plattsburgh, Poughkeepsie, Schenectady.* 2nd ed. Scarsdale, N.Y.: Rowland Mitchell, Jr., 1987. Based on 990-PF returns filed with the IRS. Main sections arranged alphabetically by foundations which made grants totaling more than $5,000 or had assets of $100,000 or more and by corporations with net earnings of at least $10 million. Entries for over 60 foundations provide names of managers, financial data, and sample grants. Entries for more than 40 corporations provide address, phone number, the names and titles of one or two executive officers, and the company's business focus. Alphabetical indexes of foundation and corporation names, as well as an index to managers. Available from Rowland L. Mitchell, see above.

New York. Mitchell, Rowland L., Jr., ed. *The Mitchell Guide to Foundations, Corporations and Their Mangers: Westchester, Including Putnam, Rockland and Orange Counties.* 2nd ed. Scarsdale, N.Y.: Rowland Mitchell, Jr., 1987. Based on 990-PF returns filed with the IRS. Main sections arranged alphabetically by foundations which made grants totaling more than $5,000 or had assets of $100,000 or more and by corporations with net earnings of at least $10 million. Entries for 214 foundations provide names of managers, financial data, and sample grants. Entries for 75 corporations provide address, phone number, the names and titles of one or two executive officers, and the company's business focus. Alphabetical indexes of foundation and corporation names, as well as an index to managers. Available from Rowland L. Mitchell, see above.

New York. Mitchell, Rowland L., Jr., ed. *The Mitchell Guide to Foundations, Corporations and Their Managers: Western New York, Including Buffalo, Jamestown, Niagara Falls, Rochester.* 2nd ed. Scarsdale, N.Y.: Rowland Mitchell, Jr., 1987. Based on 990-PF returns filed with the IRS. Main sections arranged alphabetically by foundations which made grants totaling more than $5,000 or had assets of $100,000 or more and by corporations with net earnings of at least $10 million. Entries for more than 130 foundations provide names of managers, financial data, and sample grants. Entries for 90 corporations provide address, phone number, the names and titles of one or two executive officers, and the company's business focus. Alphabetical indexes of foundation and corporation names, as well as an index to managers. Available from Rowland L. Mitchell, see above.

New York. National Center for Charitable Statistics. *Yearbook of New York State Charitable Organizations: Fund-Raising and Expense Information As Reported by Charitable, Civic, Health, Fraternal, and Other Organizations.* Washington, D.C.: Independent Sector, 1987. Directory lists the charities registered with the New York State Department of State, Office of Charities Registration as either raising or intending to raise contributions of at least $10,000 annually. The directory is arranged in three parts: an alphabetical master list, a cross-reference guide by type of organization, and a county cross-reference. The master list contains organization name and address; New York State registration number; a classification code which identifies the general organization type; date of information; and dollar amounts for direct public support, total support and revenue, payments to affiliates, program expense, management and general expense, fundraising and total expenses. Available from Independent Sector, National Center for Charitable Statistics, 1828 L Street, N.W., Suite 1200, Washington, DC 20036. (202) 223-8100.

New York. Olson, Stan, and Natividad S.H. del Pilar, eds. *New York State Foundations: A Comprehensive Directory.* New York: Foundation Center, 1988. Comprehensive directory of more than 4,500 independent, company-sponsored, and community foundations which are currently active in New York State and which have awarded grants of one dollar or more in the latest fiscal year. Arranged alphabetically by New York counties (including the five boroughs of New York City). A separate section includes 97 out-of-state foundations with funding interests in New York State. Each foundation entry includes information on address; telephone numbers; principal donor(s); assets; gifts received; expenditures, including dollar value and number of grants paid (with largest and smallest grant paid indicated); fields of interest; types of support; geographic preference; limitations; publications; application information; names of officers, principal administrators, trustees, or directors; Employer Identification Number (useful in ordering copies of the foundation's 990-PF); and a listing of sample grants, when available, to indicate the foundation's giving pattern. Indexed by donors, officers, and trustees; geographic location; types of support; broad giving interests; and foundation name. Available from the Foundation Center, 79 Fifth Avenue, Dept. I.C., New York, NY 10003. (800) 424-9836.

North Carolina.   Shirley, Anita Gunn, ed. *Grantseeking in North Carolina: A Guide to Foundation and Corporate Giving*. Raleigh, N.C.: North Carolina Center for Public Policy Research, 1985. Based on 1981 through 1983 990-PF returns filed with the IRS and questionnaires answered by 589 foundations. Main sections arranged by type of foundation; entries include financial data, trustees, sample grants, limitations, and application procedures. Alphabetical index of foundations and corporations; indexes by county, funding interest, and index of officers, directors, and trustees. Appendixes on proposal writing and corporate fundraising. Available from North Carolina Center for Public Policy Research, P.O. Box 430, Raleigh, NC 27602.

North Carolina.   Shirley, Anita Gunn, ed. *North Carolina Giving: The Directory of the State's Foundations*. Raleigh, N.C.: Capital Consortium, 1990. Descriptions of 707 private and community foundations with combined assets of $2.8 billion and annual contributions in excess of $169 million. Indexes. Capitol Consortium, P.O. Box 2918, Raleigh, NC 27602. (919) 833-4553.

North Carolina.   See also **Tennessee:** O'Donnell, Suzanna, et al. *A Guide to Funders in Central Appalachia and the Tennessee Valley*.

Ohio.   Ohio. Attorney General's Office. *Charitable Foundations Directory of Ohio*. 8th ed. Columbus, Ohio: Attorney General's Office, 1987. Directory compiled from the registration forms and annual reports of the 1,800 grantmaking charitable organizations in Ohio which represent $3.4 billion in assets and $262 million in grants. The basic information in the directory includes name of foundation, address, contact person, and telephone number; restrictions; purpose (designated with a purpose code); total assets; year of latest Attorney

General's report; total grants awarded for latest year; and the Ohio Attorney General's trust number. The directory contains both a purpose (subject area) and a county index. Available from Office of the Attorney General, Charitable Foundations Section, 30 East Broad St., 15th fl., Columbus, OH 43266-0410.

Ohio. *The Source: A Directory of Cincinnati Foundations.* Cincinnati, Ohio: Junior League of Cincinnati, 1985. Based primarily on 1982 and 1983 990-PF returns filed with the IRS and questionnaires answered by 259 foundations. Main section arranged alphabetically by foundation; entries may include financial data, sample grants, area of interest, officers and trustees, and application information. Indexed by areas of interest. Available from Junior League of Cincinnati, Regency Square, Apt. 6-F, 2334 Dana Avenue, Cincinnati, OH 45208.

Oklahoma. Streich, Mary Deane, comp. and ed. *The Directory of Oklahoma Foundations.* Oklahoma City, Okla.: Foundation Research Project, 1988. Based on information from the latest IRS 990 forms on file at the Oklahoma Medical Research Foundation, directory provides basic information on more than 240 Oklahoma foundations. Includes funding emphasis, geographic area, restrictions, financial data (assets, income, total grants, and total pledges), information on the application process and the name, address, and phone number of the contact person. Indexed by foundation name, city location, areas of funding interest, and trustees. Available from Foundation Research Project, P.O. Box 1146, Oklahoma City, OK 73101-1146.

Oregon. McPherson, Craig, comp. *The Guide to Oregon Foundations.* Portland, Oreg.: United Way of Columbia-Willamette, 1987. Based on 990-PF and 990-AR forms filed with the Oregon Attorney General's Charitable Trust Division and information supplied by more than 350 foundations. Main section arranged alphabetically by foundation within five subdivisions: general purpose foundations, special purpose foundations, student aid or scholarship funds, service clubs, and national or regional foundations with an active interest in Oregon. Entries include statement of purpose, financial data, sample grants, officers, and contact person. Appendixes include foundations ranked by asset size, by grants awarded, and by geographic focus; index of foundation names with Attorney General index numbers. Available from United Way of the Columbia-Willamette, 718 West Burnside, Portland, OR 97209. (503) 228-9131.

Pennsylvania. Kletzien, S. Damon, ed. *The Corporate Funding Guide of Greater Philadelphia.* Philadelphia: Greater Philadelphia Cultural Alliance, 1984. Contains full profiles of the charitable giving activities of 69 selected corporations and banks in the Philadelphia area. Entries provide information on business activities, number of employees, sales, profit, top officers, type of charitable support, application guidelines, and contact person. Section 2 provides a summary listing (address, contact person, telephone number) of 73 other corporations and banks in greater Philadelphia with charitable giving programs. Appendixes contain listings of the names of major advertising agencies, commercial banks, savings and loan associations, brokerage firms, CPA firms, insurance companies, law firms, and real estate agencies in greater Philadelphia; a ranking by sales volume of the 100 largest firms in the Philadelphia area; and an annotated bibliography of 33 publications on corporate giving and researching corporations. Available from Greater Philadelphia Cultural Alliance, 1718 Locust St., Philadelphia, PA 19103. (215) 735-0570.

Pennsylvania. Kletzien, S. Damon *Directory of Pennsylvania Foundations*, 3rd ed. Springfield, Pa.: Triadvocates Associated, 1986. Based primarily on 1984 990-PF returns filed with the IRS and information supplied by the more than 2,300 foundations listed in the directory. Organized in five geographical regions. Full profile entries for about 975 foundations with assets exceeding $75,000 or awarding grants totaling $5,000 or more on a discretionary basis; entries include a statement on geographical emphasis of giving, a descending listing of all grants down to $250, listing of major interest codes, application guidelines and/or statement on giving policy when available, and a list of directors, trustees, and donors. Other foundations not meeting above criteria listed by name, address, and status code only. Appendix article on broadening the foundation search. Indexes of officers, directors, trustees, and donors; major giving interests; and foundation names. Available from Triadvocates Associated, P.O. Box 336, Springfield, PA 19064. (215) 544-6927.

Pennsylvania. Kletzien, S. Damon, comp. *Directory of Pennsylvania Foundations.*Supplement. 3rd ed. Springfield, Pa.: Triadvocates Associated, 1988. This supplement to the third edition contains information on Pennsylvania foundations which filed 990-PF's for the first time since the third edition was published in July 1986. The supplement is alphabetically arranged within geographic regions. Full profiles for 216 foundations with assets exceeding $75,000 or which award grants totaling at least $5,000; all other foundation entries provide only name, address, and status code. Indexed by foundation name; officers, directors, and trustees; and major interests. Available from Triadvocates Press, P.O. Box 336, Springfield, PA 19064. (215) 544-6927.

Rhode Island. Burns, Michael E., ed. *Corporate Philanthropy in*

New England: Rhode Island. Hartford, Conn.: D.A.T.A., 1989. Based on questionnaires and telephone interviews with more than 250 corporations. Main section arranged alphabetically; entries include product, plant location, giving interests and non-cash giving, where available. Subject and index of corporations by city. Available from D.A.T.A., Inc., 30 Arbor St. North, Hartford, CT 06106. (203) 786-5225.

Rhode Island. Council for Community Services, *Directory of Grant-Making Foundations in Rhode Island.* Providence, R.I.: Council for Community Services, 1983. Based on 1980 and 1981 990-PF and 990-AR returns filed with the IRS, information from the Rhode Island Attorney General's Office and information provided by the 91 foundations listed. Main section arranged alphabetically by foundation; entries include officers and trustees, assets, total dollar amount of grants and total number of grants, statement of purpose, geographic restrictions, application information, and sample grants. Includes "Introduction to Foundations"; indexes of foundations by total dollar amount of grants made, foundations by location and by area of interest. Available from The Council for Community Services, 229 Waterman St., Providence, RI 02906.

South Carolina. Williams, Guynell, ed. *South Carolina Foundation Directory.* 3rd ed. Columbia, S.C.: South Carolina State Library, 1987. Based on 1984 through 1986 990-PF returns filed with the IRS by 196 foundations. Main section arranged alphabetically by foundation; entries include areas of interest, principal officer, assets, total grants, number of grants, range and geographic limitations. Indexed alphabetically by foundation name, location, and program interest. Available from South Carolina State Library, 1500 Senate St., P.O. Box 11469, Columbia, SC 29211. (803) 734-8666.

South Dakota. South Dakota State Library, comp. *The South Dakota Grant Directory.* Pierre, S. Dak.: South Dakota State Library, 1989. Directory produced by the South Dakota State Library contains information on more than 300 grantmaking institutions in South Dakota, including foundations, state government programs, corporate giving programs, and South Dakota scholarships. Also lists major foundations located outside the state which have shown an interest in South Dakota, and non-grantmaking foundations. Descriptions of grantmakers include name, address, and purpose statements, along with information on finances, application requirements, and eligibility/limitations. Indexed by subject and name; appendixes contain definitions of foundation types and an annotated bibliography of materials relating to foundations, student funding, grant research, and

and proposal writing. Available from South Dakota State Library, 800 Governors Drive, Pierre, SD 57501-2294. (800) 592-1841 (SD only), (605) 773-3131.

Tennessee. Memphis Bureau of Intergovernmental Management. *The Tennessee Directory of Foundations and Corporate Philanthropy.* 3rd ed. Memphis, Tenn.: City of Memphis. Bureau of Intergovernmental Management, 1985. Profiles of 58 foundations and 21 corporations and corporate foundations, based primarily on 990-PF returns filed with the IRS and questionnaires. Two main sections arranged alphabetically by foundation and alphabetically by corporation; entries include contact person, contact procedure, fields of interest, geographic limitations, financial data, officers and trustees, and sample grants. Indexes of foundation and corporations by name, fields of interest, and geographic area of giving. Appendixes of foundations giving less than $10,000 a year, and major corporations in Tennessee which employ more than 300 persons. Available from City of Memphis, Bureau of Intergovernmental Management, 125 North Mid-America Mall, Room 508, Memphis, TN 38103. (901) 528-2809.

Tennessee. O'Donnell, Suzanna, and Kim Klein, eds. *A Guide to Funders in Central Appalachia and the Tennessee Valley.* Knoxville, Tenn.: Appalachian Community Fund, 1988. Funded by the Mary Reynolds Babcock Foundation, this guide lists nearly 500 funders which give grants in the geographical region that includes northern Alabama, northern Georgia, eastern Kentucky, western North Carolina, southeastern Virginia, and the entire states of Mississippi, Tennessee, and West Virginia. The directory begins with a section on "How to Write a Grant Proposal" which includes a sample proposal and a companion cassette tape. The audiotape "How to Write a Proposal" was produced by the Carpetbag Theatre. From the several thousand foundations operating in the region, the compilers included those which met the criteria of: (1) annual grantmaking of $25,000 or assets of $500,000, and (2) a willingness to consider proposals from organizations or groups not previously funded. (Businesses and corporations are not listed unless they have their own foundation.) In addition to these foundations, religious organizations as well as foundations outside Appalachia which make grants and revolving loan funds in the region are listed in Sections 3, 4, and 5. The guide is indexed alphabetically, by interest areas, and by funders grouped within interest areas. Also included is a bibliography and a listing of the Foundation Center research collections within the region. Available from Appalachia Community Fund, 517 Union Street, Suite 206, Knoxville, TN 37902.

Texas. Herfurth, Sharon, and Karen Fagg, eds. *Directory of Dallas County Foundations*. Dallas, Tex.: Dallas Public Library, 1984. Based on 1982 and 1983 990-PF returns and information provided by the Funding Information Library and the Foundation Center on 268 foundations. Main section arranged alphabetically by foundation; entries include contact person, interests, total assets, total amount and number of grants, and officers. Appendix of Dallas foundations ranked by assets; index of foundations by giving interests and index of trustees and officers. Available from Urban Information Center, Dallas Public Library, 1515 Young St., Dallas, TX 75201. (214) 670-1487.

Texas. Logos Associates. *The Directory of the Major Texas Foundations*. Attleboro, Mass.: Logos Associates, 1986. Full profiles for 73 major foundations making grants above $400,000 in Texas, with address, telephone number, contact, foundation activities, categories of giving, financial data, application procedures, grant range and geographic area (some grants made out of state), and sample grants. Partial profiles for 33 additional foundations making less than $400,000 in grants, listing address, financial data, number and/or amount of grants made; some entries have sample grants. Name, address, and telephone numbers for 34 major Texas foundations granting $200,000 to $399,000. Includes subject index. Available from Logos Associates, 7 Park St., Room 212, Attleboro, MA 02703.

Texas. Blackwell, Dorothy and Catherine Rhodes, *Directory of Tarrant County Foundations*. 4th ed. Fort Worth, Tex.: Texas Christian University, 1989. Based on 990-PF forms filed with the IRS and foundation questionnaires. Main section arranged alphabetically by foundation; entries include financial data, officers and trustees, types of support, and application information. Indexes of foundations, trustees and officers, types of support, and fields of interest. Appendixes of foundations by asset amount and foundations by total grants, excluded and terminated foundations, and subject index. Available from Funding Information Center, Texas Christian University, Mary Couts Burnett Library, P.O. Box 32904, Fort Worth, TX 76129. (817) 921-7664.

Texas. Webb, Missy, ed. *Directory of Texas Foundations*. 10th ed. San Antonio, Tex.: Funding Information Center of Texas, 1989. A total of 1,510 private foundations, corporate giving programs, government agencies, and public charities are profiled. Directory is divided into 895 large foundations and 615 small foundations (with assets of less than $300,000 and grantmaking activity of less than $15,000). Entry information includes foundation name, emphasis (giving area), population group, restrictions, tax year of financial data, assets, total grants, grant range, application process, trustees, and contact person. Includes sections with top 100 Texas foundations in descending order by assets and by grants, excluded and terminated foundations, and a 1987 grant distribution of Texas foundations. Indexed by areas of giving, city, trustees and officers, and foundation name. Available from Funding Information Center of Texas, Inc., 507 Brooklyn, San Antonio, TX 78215. (512) 227-4333.

Texas. Webb, Missy, ed. *Directory of Texas Foundations.* Supplement. 10th ed. San Antonio, Tex.: Funding Information Center of Texas, 1989. Provides updated financial information on foundations listed in the *Directory of Texas Foundations,* 10th ed. Includes 80 foundations not previously profiled and updates on previously profiled foundations. Tables; indexes. Available from Funding Information Center of Texas, Inc., see above.

Utah. Jacobsen, Lynn Madera. *A Directory of Foundations in Utah.* Salt Lake City, Utah: University of Utah Press, 1985. Based on 1980 through 1982 990-PF returns filed with the IRS by 189 foundations in Utah, with additional information supplied by questionnaire. Main section arranged alphabetically by foundation name; entries include officers and directors, financial data, area of interest, types of support, grant analysis, and sample grants. Alphabetical index of foundations as well as index by area of interest and index of officers, directors, and advisors. Available from University of Utah Press, 101 University Services Bldg., Salt Lake City, UT 84112. (800) 444-8638, Ext. 6771.

Vermont. Burns, Michael E., ed. *Corporate Philanthropy in New England:* Vermont. Vol. 4. Hartford, Conn.: D.A.T.A., 1987. Entries for more than 125 corporate giving programs, providing address, phone number and contact, brief corporate profile and general philanthropic policies, annual cash contributions, and giving priorities. Subject and geographic indexes. Available from D.A.T.A., Inc., 30 Arbor St. North, Hartford, CT 06106. (203) 786-5225.

Virginia. See **Tennessee:** O'Donnell, Suzanna, et al. *A Guide to Funders in Central Appalachia and the Tennessee Valley.*

Washington. Washington (State). Office of Attorney General. *Charitable Trust Directory.* Olympia, Wash.: Attorney General of Washington, 1987. Based on the 1987 records in the files of the Attorney General of Washington. Includes information on more than 400 charitable organizations and trusts reporting to the Attorney General under the Washington Charitable Trust Act. Divided into two main sections: "Grantmakers" and "Grantseekers." Grantmaker entries may include statement of purpose, officers, sample grants, and financial data. Alphabetical index of all organizations appearing in the directory, and another of grantmakers only, divided into purpose categories. Available from Attorney General of Washington, 7th floor, Highways-Licenses Building, Olympia, WA 98504-8071.

West Virginia. *West Virginia Foundation Directory.* 2nd ed. Charleston, W. Va.: Kanawha County Public Library, 1987. Divided into two sections, the first half of the directory consists of 62 profiles derived from survey data and 990-PF financial data. Each profile gives the foundation's name, address, contact person, date established, and information on the foundation's giving interest, restrictions, and application procedures; lists trustees, when available, and provides a chronological list of assets and grants in dollars. The second half of the directory consists of 42 foundations which did not return their surveys; provides each foundation's name, address, and contact person, if given in the tax form, and includes the assets and grants in dollars. Final section contains updates on more than 100 foundations. Index by foundation name only. Available from Kanawha County Public Library, 123 Capitol Street, Charleston, WV 25301.

West Virginia. See also **Tennessee:** O'Donnell, Suzanna, et al. *A Guide to Funders in Central Appalachia and the Tennessee Valley.*

Wisconsin. Hopwood, Suan H., ed. *Foundations in Wisconsin: A Directory.* Milwaukee, Wis.: Marquette University Memorial Library, 1988. Contains information on 713 active grantmaking foundations. Entries include name of foundation, address, officers and directors, assets, grants paid, range, purpose, sample grants, and interests. (Lists the 50 largest foundations by grantmaking amount.) Also listed are more than 250 unprofiled grantmakers which are rated as inactive, operating, restricted, or terminated foundations. Directory includes an area of interest index, Wisconsin county index of foundations, and an officer index. Available from Marquette University Memorial Library, 1415 West Wisconsin Avenue, Milwaukee, WI 53233.

Wyoming. Darcy, Kathy, ed. *Wyoming Foundations Directory.* 3rd ed. Cheyenne, Wyoming: Laramie County Community College, 1985. Based on 990-PF and 990-AR returns filed with the IRS and a survey of more than 70 foundations listed in the directory. Main section arranged alphabetically by foundation; entries include statement of purpose and contact person when available. Also sections on foundations based out-of-state that award grants in Wyoming and a list of foundations awarding educational loans and scholarships. Index of foundations. Available from Laramie County Community College,

1400 East College Drive, Cheyenne, WY 82007. (307) 634-5853, Ext. 206.

Wyoming.   See also **Montana:** McRae, Kendall, et al. *The Montana and Wyoming Foundation Directory.*

Reprinted with permission from *National Data Book of Foundations*, Edition 14, the Foundation Center, New York, NY, 1990.

GLOSSARY

Annual report. A yearly report published by foundations and nonprofit agencies that describes their activities, grants, and financial status.

Applicant. Individual, agency, or organization seeking funds.

Award. A grant.

Awarding agency. Funding agency that makes a grant.

Award notice. Formal written notification from a funding agency to a recipient, announcing that a grant has been awarded; also called "notice of grant award."

Bidder's list. A list of qualified organizations maintained by government agencies for the purpose of sending organizations invitations to submit proposals and to bid on potential government contracts. Lists of bidders are used in determining to whom to send RFPs.

Block grant. A grant from a government funding source made as a total amount on the basis of some formula to a number of different recipients, often with relatively little control over its utilization. Revenue-sharing grants for certain general purposes are regarded as block grants.

Budget. Itemized list of expenditures and income that accompanies a narrative proposal.

Budget period. Interval of time (usually twelve months) into which a grant-project period is divided for budgetary and reporting purposes.

Business proposal. Used by some governmental grantors to refer to a separate proposal covering the budget and business aspects of the proposal, as distinguished from the technical or programmatic aspects of the proposal.

Capital grant. Grant made for major equipment and buildings as contrasted to operating expenses.

Capitation. Payment per capita; used for a grant made to an organization on the basis of a given amount for each person enrolled or served, or potentially available to be served. The total amount of such a grant is the per capita amount granted multiplied by the number of persons served.

Challenge grant. A grant that is made on the condition that the grantee raise a portion of the funds; often the same as a matching grant.

Circular A-110. Office of Management and Budget (OMB) circular that sets forth the federal standards for financial-management systems to be maintained by organizations receiving federal funds.

Commerce Business Daily. Publication of Department of Commerce that announces availability of contracts (RFPs) and recipients of contract awards from the federal government.

Community foundation. A foundation whose funds come from many different contributors and whose activities are generally limited to a particular community.

Construction grant. Grant made for and limited to construction, modernizing, or expanding a physical facility.

Contract. Legal agreement between the grantee and grantor establishing the work to be performed, products to be delivered, time schedules, financial arrangements, and other provisions or conditions governing the arrangement.

Contractor. Organization under a contract to the funder to perform specific work.

Corporate foundation. A foundation whose funds come from a corporation but which is a separate organization.

Corporate gift. A gift directly from a corporation that comes from its opening expenses or profits and is not administered through a foundation.

Cost overrun. Difference between original estimated cost and the cumulative total of a cost-reimbursable contract.

Cost-plus contract. Contract that provides for reimbursing the contractor for allowable costs that were incurred, plus a fixed fee or amount. Normally used with profit-making organizations; also known as cost-plus fixed-fee contract.

Cost proposal. Separate proposal covering the budget, financial, and business aspects of the proposal; also called business proposal.

Cost-reimbursement contract. Contract that provides for payment to the contractor on the basis of actual allowable costs or expenditures incurred in performing the scheduled work.

Cost sharing. Arrangement whereby the grantee shares in the total cost of a project; required for many federal research programs.

Demonstration grant. Grant made to support the demonstration and testing of the feasibility or piloting of a particular approach to service delivery, research, training, or technical assistance.

Direct assistance. Grant under which goods and services are furnished in lieu of cash; it can be in the form of personnel, supplies, or equipment.

Direct costs. Budget item that represents the direct expenditure of funds for salaries, fringe benefits, travel, equipment, supplies, communication, publications, and similar items.

Discretionary fund. Government funds to be allocated by a federal agency, usually on the basis of competitive selection among a number of programs and purposes rather than according to any formula; the allocation results in contracts or grants.

FAPRS. Federal Assistance Program Retrieval System, developed to provide local communities with information on federal programs.

Federal Register. Daily publication of the U.S. government that reports the rules and regulations governing various programs.

Fellowship. Grant to support individual training to enhance the individual's level of competence in a particular field.

FFP. Federal financial participation.

Fixed-price contract. Contract in which a fixed total amount is paid on the basis of delivery of a satisfactory product, regardless of the costs actually incurred by the contractor.

Formula grant. Grant in which the funds are made available on the basis of a specific formula used by the granting agency and prescribed in legislation, regulations, or policies of that agency. Formula grants may make funds available on the basis of population characteristics (e.g., two dollars for each person in a county age sixty-five and over), or on the basis of the proportion of the population in a certain area to that of the total population to be served (e.g., ABC State represents 10 percent of the U.S. total population), or on the basis of numbers of people served (e.g., twenty dollars for each person enrolled in a program).

Fringe benefits. Amount paid by the employer for various employee benefits such as social security, health insurance, retirement, and other insurances. Usually included in a budget as a percentage of total salaries.

GANTT chart. Timetable in chart form, showing the various activities included in a proposal, with indication of the length of time elapsing from the start to the end of each activity.

Grant. Sum of money comprising an award of financial assistance to recipient individuals and organizations.

Grantee. Individual, organization, or entity receiving a grant and responsible or accountable for that grant.

Grantor. Agency (government, foundation, corporation, nonprofit organization, individual) awarding a grant to a recipient.

Grant-supported activities/project. Activities specified in a grant application, contract, letter of approval, or other document that are approved by a funding agency as the basis for awarding a grant.

Grants-management officer. Official of a government funding agency or foundation who is designated as the responsible person for the business and financial aspects of a particular grant. This person is usually expected to work in collaboration with the grantor's program/project officer. The grants-management officer is the grantor's counterpart of the grantee's business and financial manager.

Guidelines. Set of general principles specified as the basis for judging a proposal. Funder's guidelines specify which requirements the proposal must meet with respect to both its content and its form.

Indirect cost. Budget item that represents costs incurred by the grantee in carrying out a program that are not readily identified as the direct expenditure of funds for goods and services, but which are necessary to facilitate and maintain the operations of the larger organizations sponsoring or carrying out the supported program. Examples are maintaining facilities, providing administration, and depreciation.

In-kind contribution. Dollar value of noncash contribution to a program by the grantee or a party other than the grantee or grantor. Such a contribution usually consists of contributed time of personnel, equipment, supplies, and rent that directly benefit the grant-supported activity.

Level of effort. Estimated amount of time of personnel required to carry out a program, project, or activity usually expressed in man-years, -months, -weeks, -days, or -hours.

Local government. Units of government below the state level such as counties, cities, towns, townships, school districts, and federally re-organized Indian tribal governments.

Local planning agencies. Known as LPAs, these are agencies designated as the official responsible recipients for certain types of grants.

Maintenance of effort. Requirement of some grantor programs that a grantee must maintain a specified level of activity and financial expenditures in a specified geographic or programmatic area in order to receive a grant. This is intended to assure that grant funds will not be used to replace or supplant funds already being expended by the grantee.

Man-years. Indicates the level of effort to be expended. A sexist term, being replaced by "person-years."

Matching. Participation by the grantee in the cost of a program on a dollar-for-dollar basis or other predetermined ratio or basis, such as 10 percent or 25 percent of the cost.

Milestones. Timetable indicating the completion of the activities or events included in a proposal.

Notice of grant award. Formal written notice from the grantor that specifies the amount of the grant, time period, and special requirements.

990-AR. Form of the annual reports that foundations submit to the Internal Revenue Service and to state attorneys general.

Offeror. Organization that is submitting a proposal on and bidding on an RFP.

Operating funds or grant. Refers to funds or a grant used for the regular operating budget of an organization; also known as grant for general purposes.

Person-years. Used to indicate the level of effort of a given person or in the aggregate for an entire project in terms of years of work to be expended. For example, "The project will require a total of six person-years over a twelve-month period."

PERT. Acronym for Program Evaluation Review Technique, which is a schedule of events and activities included in a project indicating the period of time elapsing between events and the relationship of events to each other.

Planning grant. Grant intended to support activities necessary to design and plan a particular program or project, to design and plan programs in a particular geographic area and/or a particular field of service, or to engage in interagency planning and coordination. Planning grants often include research, study, coordination, community participation, community organization, and education activities as components of the planning activities.

Principal investigator. See Program director.

Prior approval. Written permission from a granting agency (usually a governmental funder) for a grantee to expend funds or perform or modify certain activities when this is a requirement of the grantor. An approved budget is, in effect, prior approval; approval of a revised budget or written request to make program modifications is also a form of prior approval.

Private foundation. A nonprofit organization that grants funds usually from an individual, family, or corporation for social, health, educational, religious, and other charitable activities.

Program director. Individual designated by the grantee to direct the program or project being supported by the grant; also known as "project director" or "principal investigator." This person is responsible to the grantee organization for proper management and conduct of the project or program. The grantee organization is responsible to the grantor. In some unusual cases, however, project directors and principal investigators may be made directly accountable to grantors.

Program/project costs. Direct and indirect cost incurred in carrying out a grant-supported program or project. In the case of some grantors, only the cost estimated in the approved budget may be incurred by the grantee as allowable expense related to the grant.

Program or project officers. Usually refers to the official in a governmental funding agency or in a foundation who is responsible within that agency for a grant project or program. In some cases this person may, in addition to supervision of technical and program aspects of the grants, be responsible for administrative and financial aspects of the grant. This latter function is more frequently the responsibility, at least in federal agencies, of a second person (called the grants-management officer).

Program/project period. Total time over which the grant is to be expended.

Proposal. Formal written document that provides detailed information to a funder on the proposed conduct and cost of a specific program or project.

Reimbursement formula. Basis for a grantor providing funds to a grantee in cases where funds are to be granted according to some formula related to population, services rendered, or proportion of the budget to be shared by the grantee.

Research grant. Grant to support research in the form of studies, surveys, evaluations, investigations, and experimentation.

Revenue sharing. Federal program providing more or less automatic federal assistance to states and localities for broad general purposes and with limited federal control.

RFA. Acronym for request for applications, which is a formal announcement from a funding agency inviting the submission of proposals according to certain specifications. Usually results in a grant that does not set forth a specific product as do the contracts that emanate from an RFP.

RFP. Acronym for Request for Proposal, which is a formal announcement from a funding agency inviting the submission of a proposal and specifying the requirements the proposal must meet with respect to the objectives, scope of work, work plan, administration, timing, and reporting. An RFP usually results in a contract as the mechanism for conveying the funds and sets forth the specific products that are to result from the program or project.

Site visit. Visit by one or more persons responsible to the funding agency to the site of the submitter of a proposal in order to obtain additional evaluative information on the basis of firsthand observation and discussion.

Solicited proposal. Proposal that responds to an RFP or a formal invitation of a funder.

Sole source. Agency or organization considered by the funder to be the only available resource to fulfill the requirements of a proposed contract.

Stipend. Payment to an individual, usually as part of a training or fellowship program.

Technical proposal. Used by some governmental grantors to refer to the narrative proposal that covers all aspects of the proposal except the budget and financial and business information (which is to be included in a separate business proposal).

Third party. Organization or individual other than the grantee or grantor who is involved in a supported program.

Training grant. Grant to support training of staff, students, prospective employees, program participants, or designated populations.

Unobligated balance. Amount remaining of a grant at the end of the grant period against which there will be no expenses. Such balances, at the discretion of the grantor, may have to be returned, or they may be used as a deduction from the next grant (a continuation) if there is one, or carried over to the next continuation period as an addition to the next grant.

Unsolicited proposal. Proposal sent to a government foundation or other funding source that is initiated by the applicant.

Wired. Term indicating that the selection of an organization to receive a grant has been decided prior to the submission of competitive proposals.

INDEX

229